Diala's Kitchen

Plant-Forward and Pescatarian Recipes
Inspired by Home and Travel

Diala Canelo

PENGUIN

an imprint of Penguin Canada, a division of Penguin Random House Canada Limited

Canada • USA • UK • Ireland • Australia • New Zealand • India • South Africa • China

First published 2020

www.penguinrandomhouse.ca

LIBRARY AND ARCHIVES CANADA CATALOGUING IN PUBLICATION

Title: Diala's kitchen : plant-forward and pescatarian recipes inspired by home
    and travel / Diala Canelo.
Names: Canelo, Diala, author.
Identifiers: Canadiana (print) 20190133422 | Canadiana (ebook) 20190133430 |
ISBN 9780735234932 (hardcover) | ISBN 9780735234949 (HTML)
Subjects: LCSH: Vegetarian cooking. | LCSH: Pescatarian cooking. | LCGFT: Cookbooks.
Classification: LCC TX837 .C36 2020 | DDC 641.5/636—dc23

Cover and interior design by Lisa Jager
Cover and interior photography by Diala Canelo
Photography on pages ii-iii, 12, 14, and 134 by Alexa Fernando
Photography on pages 218-219 by Jim Sullivan
Photography on pages xiii, 3, and 277 by Lauren McPhillips

Printed and bound in China

10 9 8 7 6 5 4 3 2 1

Penguin
Random House
PENGUIN CANADA

To my parents, Maritza and Frank, who have been a never-ending source of love and support.

To my daughters, Isabella and Gabriela, for inspiring me every day—there is nothing I love more than being your mom. Warren, your love and determination have shown me the importance of never giving up.

Contents

Dinner

Desserts

Introduction

From the vibrant markets of Santo Domingo where I was born and grew up, to countless memories preparing and enjoying farm-to-table Sunday dinners, *Diala's Kitchen* was born from my deep and never-ending love for food and family. When I was twenty-one I moved to Montreal to study nutrition and dietetics. With its diverse and multicultural food scene, that city became the place where my passion for cooking blossomed. I loved visiting the Atwater Market in the fall and picking up fresh maple syrup to add to butternut squash soup, and in the summer months, the Jean-Talon Market was my go-to for fresh, local fruits and vegetables. Since then, farmers' markets have been a constant source of inspiration.

Beginning my Canadian food journey in Montreal was a natural way to build on my heritage and learn to develop globally inspired vegetarian and pescatarian dishes. After university, I moved to Toronto with my husband at the time and our daughter Isabella. Once relocated, I decided to become a flight attendant to fully realize the dream I had of travelling the world. I was content with my career, but I felt that something was missing. My interest in cooking, especially baking, had started to deepen in a way that I couldn't ignore. My goal became to study at Le Cordon Bleu to become a pastry chef.

In 2010, I moved to Mexico City to attend that renowned pastry school. My time there was one of the most important parts of my baking career, and it opened my senses to the beauty of the French classics. To me, learning and perfecting the techniques specific to French bread and pastry is a fundamental part of the art of baking.

When I wasn't in class, I was out exploring food markets. I lived for those daily trips to pick up fresh produce and cheese. All the flavours, colours, and textures of the produce define the soul of Mexico for me. Being able to experience the vibrancy of this cuisine in its original country showed me something very special. Mexican food is very much about the community and using native ingredients to create an experience that connects people. Being inspired in this way, while also working day and night perfecting a totally different style of cuisine, took me to a place where I knew this was what I wanted to do for the rest of my life: create recipes that highlight my passion for cooking with simple ingredients, while always making room for luscious, classically inspired desserts.

My passion for photography also ignited in Mexico as a way to document the pastries and breads that I was making in class. Friends and family saw my photos and begged me to share my recipes, and as a result, *Diala's Kitchen* came to life.

Once I graduated from Le Cordon Bleu, I knew it was time to return to the place I now consider home, Canada. I moved back to Toronto and set out to explore its incredibly diverse food scene. Along with my travels around the world, my time here has refined my style of globally infused, timeless recipes and delicious baking from scratch. Sharing my creations allows me to deeply connect with people and fuels the passion for my blog and photography. I aim to tell stories with my recipes and to inspire others to cook at home.

My Food Philosophy

I was raised in a home where healthy meals were a way of life. Everything was made from scratch, and plant-based meals were the norm, as my dad has been a vegetarian for many years. He is also a doctor who practises both traditional and alternative medicine. He taught me the importance of healthy eating and of being aware of the effect food has on our bodies. Meanwhile, my mom comes from a farming family and studied agricultural engineering. From her I learned to love fresh produce and to love spending hours in the kitchen, carefully selecting fresh ingredients and preparing simple yet flavourful meals that satisfy body and soul.

If there is something that has most influenced the way I eat, it has to be the balance my family brought to the table. We had vegetables with lunch and dinner and fresh fruit with every breakfast. But there were also pizza nights most Fridays, ice cream on hot Sunday afternoons, and sometimes a slice of fudgy chocolate cake after piano lessons—one of my favourite childhood memories. To this day I aim to eat and live in a balanced way: I choose local, in-season fruits and vegetables whenever possible, listen to my body, work out several times a week, and have a treat (or two).

The importance of listening to your body cannot be overstated. By doing so, you become aware of what's best for you. After years of being strictly vegetarian, I began craving seafood when I was pregnant with Isabella—mussels, to be exact. Since then, I have eaten fish and seafood three times a week, in addition to tons of vegetables and grains.

Growing up in Dominican Republic, a country that preserves its culture and tradition through food, has given me a deep appreciation for the dishes I've tried in my many travels. Food is not only about ingredients put together to recreate a dish. It is about the emotions a dish can evoke and the sense of community that forms when you share food with other people. This has made me realize that the way to a country's soul is through its dishes. And the way to a person's heart really is through food and the memories made while sharing a meal with loved ones.

Kitchen Staples and Equipment

A well-stocked fridge and pantry are the foundation of any meal. I like to keep some essentials on hand so I'll know I have the key ingredients necessary to bring flavour to any dish and make simple and nutritious food. From oils and vinegars to spices and nuts, I hope this list will help you stock your pantry as you cook the recipes in this book.

Staples in My Fridge

GREEK YOGURT: Not only do I use this in smoothies and to top bowls of oatmeal, but it's a great alternative to sour cream and can also be whipped into sauces.

UNSWEETENED ALMOND MILK AND COCONUT MILK: I like using these milks in smoothies and chia puddings, often infusing them with vanilla bean first.

HALLOUMI AND FETA CHEESE: Whenever I go to Athens, I bring a few blocks of halloumi and feta back home with me. I love to grill halloumi and serve it over grain bowls or salads, and I sprinkle feta cheese over soups and eggs.

PARMIGIANO-REGGIANO CHEESE: A must in my kitchen to grate over bowls of pasta, make fresh pesto, and shave on top of soups and salads.

MASCARPONE CHEESE: I fold this soft cheese into pasta dishes and use it to add creaminess to sauces.

MOZZARELLA CHEESE: I like using fresh mozzarella in all sorts of fresh and baked recipes. From Butternut Squash Frittata (page 81) to Buenos Aires Crêpes (page 179), a few pieces of torn mozzarella on top is the perfect melting cheese.

PESTO: Every summer I pick parsley and basil from my garden and make jars of Garden Pesto (page 69). In addition to using it as a sauce for pasta, it's the key ingredient in my Farro Salad with Pesto, Feta, and Walnuts (page 66). Pesto has so many uses in the kitchen. I love folding it into scrambled eggs, adding a few spoonfuls to tomato sauce, or mixing it with olive oil as a quick salad dressing.

PURE MAPLE SYRUP: I use this as a sweetener in my coffee, smoothies, and desserts, but it's also at home in savoury dishes, such as my Sesame and Maple Glazed Salmon (page 192).

MISO PASTE: Stir into soups, roasted vegetables, and marinades to add a depth of flavour.

UNSALTED BUTTER: Always on hand for baking loaves, cakes, and muffins.

FRUITS AND VEGETABLES: There is not a day when I don't either make a big salad to have with dinner, roast vegetables, or, during the winter, make vegetable-based soups. Broccoli, kale, tomatoes, sweet peppers, mushrooms, and cucumbers have a special place in our fridge. Although I don't store avocados in the fridge until after they're cut open, they definitely are a star vegetable in my kitchen. I add avocados to quesadillas, soups, salads, scrambled eggs, and my Poached Egg and Smoked Salmon Bagels (page 36). Fruits are equally important, as they are a key ingredient for smoothies, sweet sauces, and many desserts.

SALMON, HALIBUT, AHI TUNA, AND TILAPIA: Since I began following a pescatarian diet, I try to include a variety of fish in the dishes I make at home. Fish is often on our dinner table, either grilled to top salads or served with roasted vegetables.

Staples in My Pantry

PASTA: I keep both regular and whole wheat dried pasta in my pantry. From squid ink spaghetti to penne to rigatoni, nothing says comfort like a hot bowl of pasta with fresh tomato sauce or my Truffle Pasta with Mixed Mushrooms (page 183) that was inspired by my travels to Venice.

FARRO, QUINOA, FREEKEH, AND ISRAELI COUSCOUS: These grains are the base of many soups and salads throughout my book. They provide texture and a healthy addition of complex carbohydrates to my recipes.

LENTILS, CHICKPEAS, AND BLACK BEANS: Ever since I stopped eating meat, I've been adding legumes to my salads, soups, and mains, as well as making hummus and other spreads.

SEA SALT (BOTH FINE AND FLAKY): I only use sea salt in my cooking. When I want to add texture to certain dishes or roasted vegetables, I sprinkle a bit of flaky sea salt on top (I use Maldon brand).

BLACK PEPPER: I love using freshly ground pepper on soups, pastas, vegetables, and fish. I find that it pleasantly livens savoury dishes, especially fish.

OLIVE OIL, COCONUT OIL, TRUFFLE OIL, AND CHILI OIL: I use extra-virgin olive oil for cooking almost every day, and I love roasting vegetables, especially butternut squash, in coconut oil. Truffle oil adds a luscious and earthy flavour to potatoes and pasta dishes, while chili oil is a must on pizza and seafood spaghetti.

NUTS: Not only are nuts an excellent source of healthy fats, but they also add a wonderful crunch to salads, grain dishes, and bowls of oatmeal. I always keep raw (meaning unsalted, unroasted) almonds, pecans, walnuts, and hazelnuts in my freezer.

ALL-PURPOSE FLOUR, CAKE FLOUR, WHOLE WHEAT FLOUR, AND OO FLOUR: Different flours for different recipes. I like to use whole wheat flour for muffins, or mix it with all-purpose flour for pancakes. A few of my baking recipes call for cake flour, so I always have a bag on hand. In my pantry there's also Italian oo flour for those weekends when my daughters are hungry for homemade pizza.

SPICES: From saffron, cumin, oregano, and paprika to garam masala, curry powder, and chipotle chili powder, spices play such an important part in my recipes. They infuse each dish with distinctive flavours from around the world.

CHIPOTLE PEPPERS IN ADOBO SAUCE: Cans of these are always in my pantry to add delicious smoky flavour to soups, sauces, and marinades.

GOOD-QUALITY CHOCOLATE: Whenever I visit my family in Dominican Republic, I come back with bags of good-quality chocolate to use in my baking (I use dark and semisweet chocolate with a minimum of 60 percent cocoa solids). I also love Valrhona fèves—or discs—to use in cookies, cakes, and buttercream.

NATURAL ALMOND BUTTER AND PEANUT BUTTER: I use these two butters in smoothies and as a topping on oatmeal. Natural peanut butter is wonderful in peanut-based sauces to drizzle over grain bowls.

CHIA SEEDS AND HEMP HEARTS: I first started using chia seeds while living in Mexico, where they are used in everything from juices to baked goods. I add them to smoothies and salads, and I use hemp hearts in waffle and pancake batters.

VANILLA BEANS AND PURE VANILLA EXTRACT: I fell in love with Tahitian vanilla beans when I attended pastry school at Le Cordon Bleu. Vanilla was the key flavouring in pastry cream and an essential note in many of the fruit-based tarts we would make. In my pantry I keep both the beans and pure vanilla extract. They are crucial to some of the recipes you'll find in the dessert chapter and provide characteristic flavour in baking.

Equipment

FOOD PROCESSOR: This is without doubt the appliance I use the most. From pastry dough to hummus and pesto, my food processor gets a lot of use. It comes in handy to chop large quantities of nuts, and it is also a great alternative if you want to make your own nut butters but don't have a high-speed blender.

HIGH-SPEED BLENDER: A bit of an investment, but once I got mine, it became an integral tool in my kitchen. I use it to blend velvety smooth soups, nut milks, and nut butters. It blends ingredients to a smoothness that's hard to get with a regular blender.

STAND MIXER: I use mine weekly to beat egg whites for waffles and mix up muffins, buttercreams, and desserts like Chocolate and Raspberry Cake (page 255) and Lemon and Coconut Tart (page 263). A workhorse in my kitchen that simplifies so many tasks.

WAFFLE IRON: I've owned the same waffle iron for a very long time. It's been in the family through several moves around the world, and our Sunday Waffles (page 47) tradition is still going strong. Just make sure it's cleaned well after each use, and a good-quality waffle iron will last you years.

MICROPLANE GRATER: I started using one in pastry school and have kept two in my kitchen since then—one for grating garlic, ginger, and Parmesan cheese, the second one for chocolate and citrus.

FINE-MESH STRAINER: Indispensable for sifting flour, rinsing rice or quinoa, or draining smaller quantities of cooked pasta or grains.

DIGITAL KITCHEN SCALE: I use mine mostly for baking. At pastry school, we measured everything in grams. Accurate measures are crucial in baking, and weighing is much more accurate than using measuring cups. Weighing your ingredients will ensure consistent results.

SPIRALIZER: Zucchini noodles are a healthier alternative to wheat pasta, so at home I use this handy, inexpensive tool a lot, not just for zucchini but also to spiralize beets and carrots. Some models come with four or five blades that give you different thickness options.

MIXING BOWLS: From tossing salads to beating frostings to mixing batters for baking, mixing bowls get daily use in my kitchen.

POTS, PANS, AND FRYING PANS: I recently downsized my pots and pans at home, keeping only what is truly essential. Those include two 2-quart (2 L) saucepans, a 5-quart (5 L) Dutch oven, a 1-quart (1 L) small saucepan, and three oven-safe frying pans ranging from small to medium.

MEASURING CUPS: I use two sets, one for dry measures and a glass set for measuring liquids.

RUBBER SPATULAS, WOODEN SPOONS, AND WIRE WHISKS: These are essential for jobs such as folding batters, stirring custards, and whisking ingredients.

MARBLE ROLLING PIN: If your pastry gets too warm, the butter in it starts to melt, affecting flakiness and making the pastry difficult to work with. So it's crucial to keep your pastry cold while rolling it. A marble rolling pin makes this significantly easier, because of marble's natural ability to stay cool.

BENCH SCRAPER: I use this to cut triangular scones and to lift pastry dough from my counter. It's also a great tool to help clean up the counter after baking.

Santo Domingo

Lobster empanadas, rice and beans with creamy avocado and fried plantains, yuca with sautéed onions, papaya smoothies, luscious coconut flan . . . I could go on forever. The flavours of my beautiful island are bold and vibrant. Though it's been many years since I moved to Canada, every single time I visit Santo Domingo, its food welcomes me back.

The city is the oldest in the Americas, filled with history and charm. While walking along the cobblestoned streets of the picturesque Colonial Zone—the city's oldest neighbourhood—you'll come across its impressive cathedral, beautiful homes that date to the fifteenth century, vendors selling juicy tropical fruits, and iconic food spots that have been serving traditional Dominican cuisine for decades. This cuisine is a mixture of inheritances from many continents. The food of the indigenous Tainos was heavily influenced by the ingredients brought by the Spaniards when they colonized the island and by the African presence throughout the Caribbean.

Santo Domingo's gastronomy is as diverse as the island itself, and Dominican cooking has an unmistakable personality. From fried fish to *asopao de camarones*, there is such variety in its dishes. Every meal highlights the abundance of colourful local produce, locally caught seafood, and delicious tropical fruit. After all my travels around the world, it's the simplicity of Dominican cuisine that for me truly defines "food for the soul." The food of the city where I was born reminds me of long Sunday meals with my family and brings back the smell of freshly chopped cilantro, the sizzle of fish being fried, or the comforting taste of rice and pigeon peas. It reminds me of my mother's creamy pumpkin soup and how my grandmother would wait for me to return from school so that we could have lunch together.

If you have the chance to visit—and I hope you do—you'll see that the food scene in the city keeps evolving and today is more vibrant than ever, from restaurants that have given a new flair to traditional dishes to the ones that add a twist of Dominican flavour to imports like risotto and sushi.

Days before I visit my family, my mom calls to ask what I'd like to eat when I land. (*Asopao de camarones*, the Dominican shrimp and rice stew on page 197, is usually my answer.) Food has always been the way my family expresses joy and celebration. So whenever I return home, I can't help but feel nostalgic for the comforting home-cooked meals, for the turquoise seas that surround the city, and for its bougainvillea-covered courtyards.

Mexico City

Colourful, bold, boisterous, and bursting with history and tradition, Mexico City is a constant surprise to your senses. It became my home for three years and shaped the way I cook, introduced me to the world of French pastries while I attended Le Cordon Bleu, and most important, taught me to value fresh ingredients. It showed me how these ingredients gave life to Mexican dishes that have been around for centuries.

Mexico City truly embodies the farm-to-table concept. Any given Saturday, farmers' markets set up on neighbourhood plazas around the city, and people line up to fill their baskets with chilies, corn, tortillas, zucchini blossoms, fruits, vegetables, salsas, and a wealth of local cheeses. During my stay in the city, visiting the markets became part of my daily life. Seeing generations of women proudly making tortillas, sopes, and guisos while the aroma of freshly made corn tortillas filled the air is something I'll never forget. I would easily get lost for hours in the markets' life and always returned home eager to create simple recipes inspired by the ingredients I had bought.

In Mexico City, I learned that a comforting, delicious meal could be made with just a handful of fresh ingredients, like a delicious Oaxaca cheese quesadilla with zucchini blossoms and avocado, the fragrant corn tortillas, stringy cheese, and deliciously creamy avocado brought straight home from the market. Cooking with fresh ingredients is the only way when it comes to Mexican food!

The city is the largest in Latin America, and every neighbourhood has hundreds of years of rich history. From the ancient buildings in *el centro histórico*, where the Zócalo is located, to the Coyoacán, the neighbourhood where Frida Kahlo lived in the iconic Casa Azul, every corner in Mexico City celebrates art, food, and tradition.

The years I spent in Mexico opened my eyes to the vast regionality of its food, and on weekends our family would explore nearby towns. We ate our way through

San Miguel de Allende and Puebla, enjoying their chiles rellenos. We visited the iconic Oaxaca markets, spending the morning talking to vendors about their food while feasting on tlayudas, long corn tortillas topped with fresh cheese and fiery salsa. Travelling out of the city on those weekends showed me how Mexico deeply reveres its gastronomy and has built so many wonderful dishes around it.

In the last decade, Mexico City's culinary scene has exploded, and instead of looking for inspiration somewhere else, it simply looks to its roots. Bringing ancient ingredients and techniques back to life has revamped the city's culinary landscape.

If you find yourself in this colourful city, walk around the leafy parks of the Condesa and Roma neighbourhoods. Get lost among the *centro histórico*'s ancient buildings, where you'll find bakeries and restaurants that have been open for decades. Don't leave without having a cinnamon sugar–dusted churro with thick hot chocolate from El Cardenal and the tuna tostadas from Contramar. But above all, spend a morning at a farmers' market, because that's where you'll find the soul of Mexico City.

Breakfast and Brunch

There is something so calming about starting the morning with a piping hot cup of coffee while I prepare breakfast and get ready for my day. The house is quiet, the sun shines bright, and the bowl on the kitchen island is filled with fruit. My breakfasts change with the seasons. During the spring and summer, it is all about smoothie bowls or yogurt bowls, chia puddings or soft scrambled eggs. As soon as the leaves turn beautiful shades of orange and red, I simmer steel-cut oats and quinoa to make breakfast bowls topped with creamy avocado, or sweet versions with poached fruits and nuts. Winter comfort comes as fluffy pancakes, crumbly scones spiced with cinnamon or cardamom, and muffins bursting with fruit.

In our family we have a Sunday morning tradition that has been going strong for years. While my daughters and I are still in our pyjamas we make Sunday Waffles (page 47). Hot from the waffle iron and topped with juicy berries that lie on a cloud of maple whipped cream, there's no other way I'd rather start our day. After a few days of travel, to be home with my family and make them brunch is one of my life's biggest treasures.

Chia Seed Pudding Parfait with Berries and Granola

Serves 2

When I lived in Mexico City, there was not a café in town that didn't serve chia pudding. After all, chia seeds are native to southern Mexico and used in everything from baked goods to juices. But I like chia seeds most in this breakfast staple I enjoy at home: a creamy pudding full of fibre and healthy fats. I like layering the chia seeds with fresh berries, but feel free to use your favourite fruits.

2 cups (500 mL) unsweetened almond milk

2 tablespoons (30 mL) pure maple syrup

1 teaspoon (5 mL) pure vanilla extract

⅛ teaspoon (0.5 mL) sea salt

½ cup (125 mL) chia seeds

1 cup (250 mL) mixed fresh berries (such as blueberries, raspberries, strawberries)

¼ cup (60 mL) pomegranate seeds

6 tablespoons (90 mL) Maple Cinnamon Granola (page 20)

¼ cup (60 mL) natural coconut chips

1. In a medium bowl, stir together the almond milk, maple syrup, vanilla, salt, and chia seeds until well combined. Let stand for 10 minutes.

2. Stir the chia seed mixture again, then transfer to two 2-cup (500 mL) glass jars. Cover and store in the fridge overnight.

3. In the morning, top the chia seed pudding with fresh berries, pomegranate seeds, maple cinnamon granola, and coconut chips.

Maple Cinnamon Granola

Makes 12 cups (3 L)

If you walk into my kitchen, odds are you'll find a big jar of my maple cinnamon granola. It's a staple in our home, and most mornings we sprinkle it over bowls of yogurt and berries, top smoothies, or sprinkle it over muffins before baking. I've used my favourite nuts in this recipe, but feel free to use any nuts you have on hand. I often bring a jar with me on my travels to have as a snack or a quick breakfast on the go.

6 cups (1.5 L) large-flake rolled oats

1 cup (250 mL) raw almonds

1 cup (250 mL) raw macadamia nuts

1 cup (250 mL) raw pecans

1 cup (250 mL) raw cashews

1 cup (250 mL) raw sunflower seeds

1 cup (250 mL) raw pepitas

½ cup (125 mL) chia seeds

1 cup (250 mL) pure maple syrup

¼ cup (60 mL) coconut oil, melted

2 tablespoons (30 mL) cinnamon

2 teaspoons (10 mL) pure vanilla extract (or ½ vanilla bean, split lengthwise and seeds scraped)

2 cups (500 mL) unsweetened dried cranberries

1 cup (250 mL) unsweetened shredded coconut

½ cup (125 mL) hemp hearts

1. Position racks in the upper and lower thirds of the oven. Preheat the oven to 375°F (190°C). Line 2 baking sheets with parchment paper.

2. In a large bowl, stir together the oats, almonds, macadamia nuts, pecans, cashews, sunflower seeds, pepitas, and chia seeds.

3. In a small bowl, stir together the maple syrup, coconut oil, cinnamon, and vanilla.

4. Add the maple syrup mixture to the oat mixture and stir with a wooden spoon until the nuts and oats are thoroughly coated.

5. Divide the granola mixture equally between the prepared baking sheets and spread it evenly. Bake, stirring the granola every 5 minutes and switching sheets top to bottom and front to back halfway, until golden brown, about 35 minutes.

6. Place the baking sheets on racks and let cool for 20 minutes. Add the cranberries, coconut, and hemp hearts and stir to combine. Store in a covered container at room temperature for up to 1 month.

Acai and Granola Bowl

The first time I had an acai bowl, I was in Hawaii and on my way to the beach, and I stopped by a café to grab one to go. Since then, on a hot summer day, you'll find me whipping one up at home and topping it with local fresh berries, my maple cinnamon granola, and coconut chips.

Acai, a fruit grown in Brazil, is a bit tart, but adding bananas to your blend balances it out. Trust me, you'll come back to this often when the weather gets warm.

2 cups (500 mL) water or coconut water

2 packages (3½ ounces/100 g each) frozen acai purée (I use Sambazon)

1 medium banana, coarsely chopped

Toppings

1 cup (250 mL) Maple Cinnamon Granola (page 20)

½ cup (125 mL) mixed fresh berries (such as blueberries, blackberries, strawberries)

1 kiwi, peeled and sliced

1 medium banana, sliced

⅓ cup (75 mL) natural coconut chips

1. In a high-speed blender, combine the water, acai purée, and banana. Blend until smooth, about 1 minute.

2. Pour the acai mixture into bowls and top with the maple cinnamon granola, berries, kiwi, banana, and coconut chips.

Blueberry Baked Oatmeal

Serves 6

Blueberry Sauce

1 cup (250 mL) fresh orange
juice

½ cup (125 mL) + 2 tablespoons
(30 mL) water, divided

2 cups (500 mL) fresh or
thawed frozen blueberries

3 tablespoons (45 mL) pure
maple syrup

1 teaspoon (5 mL) pure vanilla
extract

1½ teaspoons (7 mL)
cornstarch

Baked Oatmeal

2 cups (500 mL) large-flake
rolled oats

½ cup (125 mL) raw pecans,
toasted, divided

1 teaspoon (5 mL) baking
powder

½ teaspoon (2 mL) ground
cardamom

½ teaspoon (2 mL) cinnamon

½ teaspoon (2 mL) sea salt

2 eggs

2½ cups (625 mL) 2% milk or
unsweetened almond milk

¼ cup (60 mL) pure maple
syrup

3 tablespoons (45 mL) unsalted
butter, melted and cooled,
divided

2 teaspoons (10 mL) pure
vanilla extract

½ cup (125 mL) fresh or frozen
blueberries

Plain full-fat Greek yogurt, for
serving (optional)

It was winter when a group of friends and I stopped at a café in Barcelona's El Born neighbourhood. After planning out our day, we decided to share a few dishes, in true Barcelona style. I chose a piping hot baked oatmeal that was served with syrupy quinces, toasted walnuts, and crème anglaise. Since then, baked oatmeal has been a breakfast staple in my kitchen—especially once the weather turns cold. Feel free to top with a dusting of icing sugar as shown—but totally optional. The blueberry sauce is also great on top of my Sunday Waffles (page 47).

1. Position a rack in the middle of the oven. Preheat the oven to 375°F (190°C). Generously butter an 8-inch (2 L) square baking dish.

2. To make the blueberry sauce: In a medium saucepan, bring the orange juice and ½ cup (125 mL) of the water to a boil. Reduce the heat to medium-low, then add the blueberries, maple syrup, and vanilla. Stir to combine.

3. In a small cup, stir together the cornstarch and the remaining 2 tablespoons (30 mL) water. Stir the cornstarch mixture into the blueberries and cook, stirring occasionally, until thickened, about 8 minutes. Pour the blueberry sauce into a glass jar to cool.

4. To make the baked oatmeal: In a medium bowl, stir together the oats, ¼ cup (60 mL) of the pecans, baking powder, cardamom, cinnamon, and salt.

5. In another medium bowl, whisk together the eggs, milk, maple syrup, half of the melted butter, and vanilla. Stir in the blueberries. Pour the egg mixture into the oat mixture and stir until combined.

6. Pour the oatmeal mixture into the prepared baking dish and top evenly with the remaining ¼ cup (60 mL) pecans. Bake for 35 minutes, or until the top is golden brown and the oatmeal is set. Let cool for 2 minutes, then drizzle the remaining melted butter over the oatmeal.

7. Serve in bowls, topped with the blueberry sauce and yogurt, if using.

Steel-Cut Oatmeal with Maple Grilled Pears and Walnuts

Serves 4

1 cup (250 mL) steel-cut oats

2 cups (500 mL) water

1 cup (250 mL) unsweetened almond milk, more for serving

½ teaspoon (2 mL) cinnamon

¼ teaspoon (1 mL) ground cardamom

¼ teaspoon (1 mL) sea salt

1½ teaspoons (7 mL) unsalted butter

¼ cup (60 mL) pure maple syrup

2 firm-ripe Bartlett pears, cut in half and cored

½ cup (125 mL) raw walnuts, toasted

Plain full-fat Greek yogurt, for serving (optional)

Dublin is one of my favourite cities in the world. Its friendly people, history-filled streets, and vibrant food scene always make me want to return. During one of my visits, I stopped by my favourite spot in the city. The Fumbally is an eclectic café, serving wholesome food that's mostly plant-based. Luca, one of the owners, has a passion for fresh ingredients, and the kitchen serves dishes that are vibrant and wholesome. I tried a hearty steel-cut oatmeal topped with nuts and stewed fruit. This is my version of that soul-comforting breakfast.

Steel-cut oatmeal, cooked with nutty almond milk and spices, is the perfect way to start your day—especially if you top a steaming bowl with grilled pears, a dollop or two of Greek yogurt, and fragrant toasted walnuts.

1. In a medium saucepan, combine the oats, water, almond milk, cinnamon, cardamom, and salt. Bring to a boil over medium heat. Reduce the heat to low and simmer for 25 minutes, without stirring. The oats will not be fully cooked.

2. In a medium frying pan, melt the butter over medium heat. Add the maple syrup and cook until bubbly, about 2 minutes. Add the pears, cut side down, and cook until brown, about 2 minutes. Turn the pears and cook until brown, about 2 minutes more. Set aside on a plate.

3. Stir in the oat mixture and cook, stirring occasionally, until the oats are tender, about 10 minutes.

4. To serve, divide the oatmeal among bowls. Top each bowl with a pear half, toasted walnuts, a splash of almond milk, and a dollop of yogurt, if using.

Overnight Maple-Banana Oats

Serves 2

Sign me up for any breakfast that helps make mornings easier. Overnight banana oats to the rescue! Prep before going to bed and have the most delicious breakfast waiting for you in the morning. Spiced with a bit of cinnamon and topped with coconut chips, these oats are bound to start your morning the right way. You can also make these in small mason jars for a breakfast or snack on the go.

2 cups (500 mL) unsweetened almond milk

2 tablespoons (30 mL) natural almond butter

2 teaspoons (10 mL) pure maple syrup

⅛ teaspoon (0.5 mL) sea salt

½ teaspoon (2 mL) cinnamon

1 cup (250 mL) large-flake rolled oats

¼ cup (60 mL) chia seeds

1 banana, sliced

Toppings

¼ cup (60 mL) plain full-fat Greek yogurt

1 banana, sliced

2 tablespoons (30 mL) sliced raw almonds, toasted

2 tablespoons (30 mL) natural coconut chips

Whole flax seeds (optional)

Chia seeds (optional)

Hemp hearts (optional)

1. In a high-speed blender, combine the almond milk, almond butter, maple syrup, salt, and cinnamon. Blend until frothy and smooth.

2. Pour the almond milk mixture into a medium bowl. Add the oats, chia seeds, and sliced banana. Stir until well combined. Divide evenly between two 2-cup (500 mL) glass jars, cover, and let rest in the fridge overnight.

3. In the morning, top the oat mixture with yogurt, sliced banana, almonds, coconut chips, and any additional toppings, if using.

Quinoa Porridge with Caramelized Bananas and Figs

Serves 2

1 cup (250 mL) white quinoa, rinsed

1½ cups (375 mL) unsweetened almond milk, divided, more for serving

½ cup (125 mL) water

1 teaspoon (5 mL) pure vanilla extract

½ teaspoon (2 mL) cinnamon

2 teaspoons (10 mL) pure liquid honey

1 tablespoon (15 mL) unsalted butter

2 tablespoons (30 mL) pure maple syrup

2 medium bananas, cut in half lengthwise

6 figs, cut in half lengthwise

½ cup (125 mL) raw walnuts, toasted

One time when I was in San Francisco, where farmers' markets are everywhere, baskets of figs adorned every stall. I discovered that when they're in season, fresh figs are incorporated into dishes throughout the city. From grilled figs over French toast to clafoutis to granola bowls, this ancient fruit is treated like a superstar, being the highlight on menus at some of my favourite cafés, such as Tartine Bakery.

Inspired by the bounty I saw in San Francisco, back home I made this nutty quinoa porridge topped with caramelized figs in maple syrup. The figs are slightly crunchy on the cut side, while juicy and soft in the inside. These caramelized figs have become my fruit of choice to top a nice warm bowl of any kind of porridge.

1. In a medium saucepan, combine the quinoa, 1 cup (250 mL) of the almond milk, water, vanilla, and cinnamon. Bring to a boil over medium-high heat. Reduce the heat to low, cover with a lid, and simmer for 12 to 14 minutes, until the quinoa is tender and has absorbed most of the liquid. Remove from the heat and stir in the honey and the remaining ½ cup (125 mL) almond milk. Cover and keep warm.

2. In a medium frying pan, melt the butter over medium heat and cook just until lightly browned. Add the maple syrup, then add the bananas and cook, without stirring, for 1 minute per side or until golden brown. Transfer the bananas to a plate and cover loosely with foil to keep warm.

3. Return the pan (no need to wipe it clean) to medium heat and add the figs, cut side down. Cook until caramelized, about 1 minute, without stirring or turning.

4. To serve, divide the quinoa mixture between bowls and top with the caramelized bananas, caramelized figs, toasted walnuts, and more almond milk, if needed.

Berry, Almond, and Yogurt Muffins

Makes 12 muffins

Where I live in Canada, farmers' markets can be found from spring through fall. Going to my local market and returning home with fresh fruit is a summer ritual that I always look forward to. If I find raspberries and blueberries, I bring back a few baskets with the sole intention of making these muffins for the week and love adding chia seeds to the batter for an extra boost of fibre and antioxidants. Chock full of berries and with a tender crumb, these muffins are perfect with a latte, and in my house they're a favourite snack for school and work.

1 cup (250 mL) whole wheat flour

1 cup (250 mL) all-purpose flour

⅔ cup (150 mL) granulated sugar

¼ cup (60 mL) large-flake rolled oats

1 tablespoon (15 mL) chia seeds

1½ teaspoons (7 mL) baking soda

1 teaspoon (5 mL) baking powder

1 teaspoon (5 mL) cinnamon

1 cup (250 mL) fresh or frozen raspberries

1 cup (250 mL) fresh or frozen blueberries

2 eggs

1 cup (250 mL) buttermilk

½ cup (125 mL) canola oil

2 tablespoons (30 mL) plain full-fat Greek yogurt

1 teaspoon (5 mL) pure vanilla extract

3 tablespoon (45 mL) raw sliced almonds

1. Position a rack in the middle of the oven. Preheat the oven to 375°F (190°C). Line a muffin tin with paper liners.

2. In a medium bowl, stir together the whole wheat flour, all-purpose flour, sugar, oats, chia seeds, baking soda, baking powder, and cinnamon. Add the raspberries and blueberries and carefully fold them into the flour mixture.

3. In another medium bowl, whisk together the eggs, buttermilk, canola oil, yogurt, vanilla, and almonds.

4. Pour the buttermilk mixture into the flour mixture and gently stir together just until combined.

5. Fill the muffin cups about three-quarters full. Bake until golden brown and a toothpick inserted in the centre of a muffin comes out clean, about 25 minutes, rotating the muffin tin halfway through.

6. Transfer to a rack and let cool in the tin for 15 minutes. Tip the muffins out onto the rack. Serve warm or at room temperature. (I like them warm.) Store in a covered container at room temperature for up to 3 days or in the freezer for up to 1 month.

Banana, Walnut, and Blueberry Muffins

Makes 12 muffins

1½ cups (375 mL) whole wheat flour

1 tablespoon (15 mL) chia seeds

1½ teaspoons (7 mL) baking soda

½ teaspoon (2 mL) cinnamon

¼ teaspoon (1 mL) sea salt

1½ cups (375 mL) fresh or frozen blueberries

¾ cup (175 mL) coarsely chopped raw walnuts

2 very ripe medium bananas

1 egg

½ cup (125 mL) canola oil

½ cup (125 mL) pure maple syrup

3 tablespoons (45 mL) plain full-fat Greek yogurt

1 teaspoon (5 mL) pure vanilla extract

½ cup (125 mL) large-flake rolled oats

When my family and I lived in Mexico City, I started baking banana muffins for my daughters as a lunch-box treat. One day I decided to add a handful of juicy blueberries and some maple syrup. The muffins were an instant hit, and from that day on I've always added these two ingredients. I think the maple syrup reminded them of Canada.

The crumb on these muffins is soft and delicate, while the blueberries and walnuts add crunch and layers of flavour. The fragrant maple syrup gives them a perfect touch of sweetness. At home in Canada, these are on repeat during the summer months, when wild blueberries are available near our family cottage in northern Ontario.

1. Position a rack in the middle of the oven. Preheat the oven to 375°F (190°C). Line a muffin tin with paper liners.

2. In a medium bowl, whisk together the whole wheat flour, chia seeds, baking soda, cinnamon, and salt. Carefully stir in the blueberries and walnuts.

3. In another medium bowl, mash the bananas. Whisk in the egg, canola oil, maple syrup, yogurt, and vanilla until well blended.

4. Pour the banana mixture into the flour mixture and gently stir just until combined.

5. Fill the muffin cups about three-quarters full. Top each muffin with a sprinkle of oats. Bake until puffed and golden brown and a toothpick inserted in the centre of a muffin comes out clean, about 25 minutes, rotating the muffin tin halfway through.

6. Transfer to a rack and let cool in the tin for 10 minutes. Tip the muffins out onto the rack. Serve warm or at room temperature. Store in a covered container at room temperature for up to 3 days or in the freezer for up to 1 month.

Poached Egg and Smoked Salmon Bagels

Serves 2

Every trip to Dublin I end up at a tiny fish store near Grafton Street, where the owner is always giving you pieces of all kinds of smoked fish to try. I buy the most flavourful smoked salmon there. It's never overly salty, and there is a delicate buttery flavour to it that makes it perfect with poached eggs, cream cheese, creamy avocado, and fresh chives. Inspired by that little fish store, this is the most requested breakfast in our home on Saturday mornings, especially when served with thinly sliced red onions. It's simple to make yet impressive enough to serve friends for brunch.

½ cup (125 mL) cream cheese, softened

1 tablespoon (15 mL) chopped fresh chives

1 tablespoon (15 mL) white vinegar

2 eggs

2 bagels

8 ounces (225 g) thinly sliced smoked salmon

1 avocado, pitted, peeled, and sliced

2 green onion (white and light green parts only), chopped

¼ cup (60 mL) thinly sliced red onion (optional)

1 tablespoon (15 mL) drained capers (optional)

1. In a small bowl, stir together the cream cheese and chives.

2. To poach the eggs, fill a medium saucepan about two-thirds with water and bring to a slow boil. Add the vinegar and reduce the heat to a simmer. Crack 1 egg into a ramekin or small bowl. Carefully place the edge of the bowl close to the simmering water and gently slip the egg into the water. Repeat with the remaining egg. Simmer for 3 minutes. The egg yolks will be slightly runny, which is how you want them.

3. Use a slotted spoon to lift the poached eggs out of the water and place them on a plate lined with paper towels.

4. Toast the bagels and spread the chive cream cheese on each cut side.

5. Top the bottom half of each bagel with a few slices of smoked salmon, a poached egg, sliced avocado, green onions, sliced red onions, and capers, if using. Top each with the other half of the bagel.

Soft Scrambled Eggs on Toast with Grilled Spring Vegetables

Serves 2

After spending two weeks in Melbourne and going for brunch every day, I learned two things: Australians take their breakfast seriously, and they take simple avocado toast to another level. Each café my partner, Warren, and I visited had endless avocado toast options. One of my favourites was topped with eggs and the softest grilled halloumi cheese. My take adds pan-grilled asparagus and juicy vine-ripened tomatoes, with a bit of truffle oil on the eggs, because let's be honest, truffle oil makes everything better.

2 eggs

Sea salt and pepper

½ teaspoon (2 mL) unsalted butter

½ teaspoon (2 mL) truffle oil

1 tablespoon (15 mL) extra-virgin olive oil

6 asparagus spears, trimmed

6 cherry tomatoes

2 thick slices halloumi cheese

1 clove garlic, cut in half

2 slices sourdough bread or your favourite bread, toasted

½ avocado, pitted, peeled, and sliced

¼ teaspoon (1 mL) red chili flakes (optional)

1. In a small bowl, whisk the eggs with a pinch each of salt and pepper.

2. Heat a medium frying pan over medium heat. Add the butter and let it melt for about 30 seconds. Add the truffle oil and reduce the heat to low, pour in the whisked eggs, and cook, stirring often, until the eggs are softly set and still slightly runny. Transfer the eggs to a plate and cover loosely with foil to keep them warm. Wipe the pan clean.

3. In the same pan, heat the olive oil over medium heat. Add the asparagus and tomatoes and cook for 3 minutes, turning the vegetables halfway through. Transfer the vegetables to a plate and cover loosely with foil to keep them warm. Wipe the pan clean.

4. Return the pan to medium heat. Add the halloumi and cook for 1 minute per side or until golden brown. Remove from the heat.

5. Rub the cut side of the garlic on the toast, then discard. Top each slice of toast with the asparagus, tomatoes, halloumi, scrambled eggs, and avocado. Sprinkle with chili flakes, if using, and serve.

Huevos Rancheros

Serves 2

So much of my inspiration in the kitchen comes from when my daughters and I lived in Mexico City. When it comes to breakfast, huevos rancheros were a big part of our weekend brunch. We would go out to our favourite neighbourhood restaurant, where the aroma of freshly made corn tortillas filled the air, and start our Saturday in the best way possible.

Bathed in a fiery tomato sauce and topped with dollops of refried black beans, these huevos rancheros are the ones I make at home when the craving for a hearty Mexican breakfast strikes.

1 can (19 ounces/540 mL) black beans, drained and rinsed

1 cup (250 mL) tightly packed chopped fresh cilantro leaves, divided

5 tablespoons (75 mL) extra-virgin olive oil, divided

1 teaspoon (5 mL) chipotle peppers in adobo sauce

⅓ cup (75 mL) water

¼ teaspoon (1 mL) sea salt

2 cloves garlic, minced

1 can (14 ounces/398 mL) fire-roasted tomatoes

½ teaspoon (2 mL) ancho chili powder

4 eggs

4 corn tortillas

¾ cup (175 mL) crumbled cotija or feta cheese

1 avocado, pitted, peeled, and sliced

1. In a blender, combine the black beans, ½ cup (125 mL) of the cilantro, 1 tablespoon (15 mL) of the olive oil, chipotle, water, and salt. Blend until smooth, about 1 minute.

2. In a small saucepan, heat 1 tablespoon (15 mL) of the olive oil over medium heat. Add the garlic and cook, stirring often, until golden, about 1 minute. Pour in the tomatoes, sprinkle the mixture with chili powder, and cook, stirring often, for 3 minutes. Remove from the heat and set aside, keeping warm.

3. In a medium frying pan, heat 1 tablespoon (15 mL) of the olive oil over medium heat. Add the black bean mixture and cook, stirring constantly, for 2 minutes, Transfer to a plate and cover with foil to keep warm. Wipe the pan clean.

4. In the same pan, heat the remaining 2 tablespoons (30 mL) olive oil over medium-high heat. Carefully crack the eggs into the pan, leaving space between each egg. Cook for 3 to 4 minutes, or until the whites are cooked and no longer translucent and the yolks are still runny. Transfer to a plate. Cover loosely with foil to keep warm. Wipe the pan clean.

5. In the same pan over medium-high heat, toast the tortillas, about 2 minutes per side. A few charred spots are okay.

6. To serve, top each tortilla with refried beans, a fried egg, tomato sauce, cheese, and avocado, and sprinkle with the remaining cilantro.

Mashed Plantains with Fried Eggs

Serves 2

If you ask any Dominican what is their breakfast of choice, be prepared to hear *mangú de plátanos*. It is basically mashed plantains, a favourite in every house, and the toppings vary from fried or scrambled eggs to fried local cheese to red onions. Since this is a country rich with avocado trees, a few slices usually make it into this delicious breakfast dish. It's what I crave most when I miss my family and the first breakfast I need to have as soon as I arrive for a visit.

2 large plantains, peeled and cut in half lengthwise

½ red onion, thinly sliced

¼ cup (60 mL) white vinegar

2 tablespoons (30 mL) extra-virgin olive oil or unsalted butter, divided

¼ teaspoon (1 mL) sea salt

¼ teaspoon (1 mL) freshly cracked pepper

2 tablespoons (30 mL) vegetable oil

2 eggs

1 avocado, pitted, peeled, and sliced

1. Bring a large pot of salted water to a boil. Add the plantains and boil until fork-tender, about 25 minutes. Drain the plantains, reserving ½ cup (125 mL) of the cooking water.

2. Meanwhile, place the red onion in a small bowl and cover with the vinegar.

3. Transfer the plantains to a medium bowl and add the reserved cooking water, 1 tablespoon (15 mL) of the olive oil, salt, and pepper. Mash the plantains to the consistency of mashed potatoes.

4. In a medium frying pan, heat the vegetable oil over medium heat. Drain the red onions and discard the vinegar. Add the onions to the pan and cook, stirring often, until soft and translucent, about 5 minutes. Transfer to a plate.

5. In the same pan (no need to wipe clean), heat the remaining 1 tablespoon (15 mL) olive oil over medium heat. Carefully crack the eggs into the pan, leaving space between each egg. Cook for 3 to 4 minutes, or until the whites are cooked and no longer translucent and the yolks are still runny. (I prefer the eggs over easy for this dish.)

6. To serve, divide the mashed plantain between plates and top with a fried egg, cooked onions, and a few slices of avocado. Season with salt and pepper to taste.

Tip Plantains are native to Southeast Asia and the Caribbean. They are a member of the banana family, but starchier and lower in sugar, with a flavour similar to potatoes. You can find them at most large grocery stores, near the potatoes and squash.

Quinoa, Egg, and Halloumi Bowls

Serves 2

Breakfast bowls are a sure way to serve up something deliciously satisfying. A few years ago, while sitting at a café in Aegina, Greece, I had a breakfast bowl topped with the softest grilled halloumi cheese and tangy Kalamata olives. The weather was glorious and warm, and we were surrounded by ancient olive trees. This recipe gathers some of my favourite ingredients to top a bowl of quinoa that will have you set for brunch.

Though halloumi cheese is the star of this bowl, you can instead use crumbled feta or goat cheese.

1 cup (250 mL) white quinoa, rinsed

2 cups (500 mL) water

½ teaspoon (2 mL) sea salt

2 tablespoons (30 mL) extra-virgin olive oil, divided

10 cherry tomatoes, cut in half

2 cups (500 mL) tightly packed baby spinach

2 eggs

4 thick slices halloumi cheese

1 avocado, pitted, peeled, and sliced

Freshly cracked pepper

1. In a medium saucepan, combine the quinoa, water, and salt. Bring to a boil over medium-high heat. Reduce the heat to low, cover with a lid, and simmer for 12 to 14 minutes, until the quinoa is tender and has absorbed all the water. Remove from the heat and fluff with a fork. Let sit, covered, until ready to use.

2. In a medium frying pan, heat 1 tablespoon (15 mL) of the olive oil over medium heat. Add the tomatoes and cook until blistered, about 3 minutes. Transfer the tomatoes to a small bowl. Wipe the pan clean.

3. To the same pan, add the spinach and cook until slightly wilted. Transfer the spinach to a plate. Cover loosely with foil to keep warm.

4. In the same pan (no need to wipe clean), heat the remaining 1 tablespoon (15 mL) olive oil over medium heat. Carefully crack the eggs into the pan, leaving space between each egg. Cook for 3 to 4 minutes, or until the whites are cooked and no longer translucent and the yolks are still runny. Transfer the fried eggs to the plate with the spinach. Wipe the pan clean.

5. Return the pan to medium heat. Add the halloumi and cook for 1 minute per side.

6. To serve, divide the warm quinoa between bowls. Top with the tomatoes, spinach, eggs, halloumi, and avocado. Season with salt and pepper to taste.

Sunday Waffles with Maple Vanilla Whipped Cream

Serves 4

Sunday mornings at home are made for waffles. Our favourite tradition started years ago, when my daughters were young, and it's still going strong. We usually eat them while still in our pyjamas, catching up on our week. When we lived in Mexico City, I would often top our waffles with fresh mango, pineapple, and a dusting of cinnamon sugar, but at home we top our waffles with fresh berries and maple vanilla whipped cream. It's moments like these that make time in the kitchen so worthwhile.

Sunday Waffles

2 eggs, separated

2 cups (500 mL) 2% milk

½ cup (125 mL) unsalted butter, melted, more for the waffle iron

1 teaspoon (5 mL) pure vanilla extract

1 cup (250 mL) whole wheat flour

1 cup (250 mL) all-purpose flour

1 tablespoon (15 mL) granulated sugar

1 teaspoon (5 mL) baking powder

Pinch of sea salt

Maple Vanilla Whipped Cream

1 cup (250 mL) whipping (35%) cream

2 teaspoons (10 mL) pure maple syrup

1 teaspoon (5 mL) pure vanilla extract

For serving

Mixed fresh berries (such as blueberries, raspberries, strawberries)

Pure maple syrup

Icing sugar, for dusting (optional)

1. Preheat the waffle iron on high heat. Preheat the oven to 200°F (100°C). Line a baking sheet with parchment paper.

2. To make the Sunday waffles: In a large bowl, whisk together the egg yolks, milk, melted butter, and vanilla.

3. In a medium bowl, combine the whole wheat flour, all-purpose flour, sugar, baking powder, and salt.

4. Add the flour mixture to the egg mixture. Using a rubber spatula, fold just until the flour is moistened.

5. In a medium bowl, beat the egg whites until they form stiff peaks. Using a rubber spatula, fold half of the egg whites into the batter, then fold in the remaining egg whites. The batter will be thin, but the egg whites will add airiness to the waffles. Set aside.

6. To make the maple vanilla whipped cream: In a large bowl, combine the cream, maple syrup, and vanilla. Beat until soft peaks form.

7. Brush both sides of the waffle iron with a thin coating of melted butter. (Grease the waffle iron even if it is nonstick.) Cook the waffles in batches, using about ⅓ cup (75 mL) of batter per waffle, until they are crisp and brown, about 4 minutes. Transfer to the baking sheet and keep warm in the oven. Repeat until all the batter is used.

8. Serve the waffles topped with a dollop of maple vanilla whipped cream, fresh berries, maple syrup, and a dusting of icing sugar, if using.

Chia and Banana Pancakes

Serves 4 to 6

At home, Sundays are made for waffles, but once in a while we switch it up for these chia and banana pancakes. The bananas in the batter make them fluffy and also add their natural sweetness. When making pancakes or waffles, I like using a combination of flours and adding chia seeds and hemp hearts for extra nutrition. Top these with berries, more bananas, and a generous pour of maple syrup.

2 eggs

1 cup (250 mL) 2% milk

1 teaspoon (5 mL) pure vanilla extract

¼ cup + 2 teaspoons (70 mL) unsalted butter, melted

1 medium banana, mashed

1 cup (250 mL) all-purpose flour

¼ cup (60 mL) whole wheat flour

4 teaspoons (20 mL) baking powder

1 tablespoon (15 mL) granulated sugar

½ teaspoon (2 mL) sea salt

1 tablespoon (15 mL) chia seeds

1 tablespoon (15 mL) hemp hearts

For serving

2 bananas, sliced

2 cups (500 mL) mixed fresh berries (such as raspberries, blueberries, strawberries)

Pure maple syrup

2 tablespoons (30 mL) icing sugar, for dusting (optional)

1. Preheat the oven to 200°F (100°C). Line a baking sheet with parchment paper.

2. In a medium bowl, whisk together the eggs, milk, vanilla, and melted butter. Stir in the mashed bananas with a spatula until thoroughly mixed.

3. In another medium bowl, sift together the all-purpose flour, whole wheat flour, baking powder, sugar, and salt. Stir in the chia seeds and hemp hearts.

4. Pour the egg mixture into the flour mixture and gently fold with a rubber spatula. Take care not to overmix—there should be some bits of flour in the mixture.

5. Grease a medium frying pan or griddle with butter and set over medium heat. When the pan is hot, drop about ¼ cup (60 mL) batter into the pan. Make more pancakes, without overcrowding the pan.

6. Once bubbles appear on the top, flip the pancakes and cook until golden brown on the bottom, about 1 minute more. Transfer to the prepared baking sheet and keep warm in the oven while you cook the remaining pancakes.

7. Serve the pancakes topped with sliced banana, berries, and maple syrup. Dust with icing sugar, if using.

Piña Colada French Toast

Serves 4

As a child in Dominican Republic, whenever I went out to brunch with my parents I would ask for a virgin piña colada. Two of my favourite fruits, coconut and pineapple, combined into one delicious drink, always with a drizzle of Dominican vanilla.

Inspired by those flavours from home, this French toast was born. Coconut milk in the batter makes it creamier and with a bit of cinnamon provides an extraordinary flavour with a topping of grilled pineapple, bananas, and coconut chips.

1 can (14 ounces/400 mL) full-fat coconut milk

1 cup (250 mL) 2% milk

5 eggs

1 tablespoon (15 mL) pure vanilla extract (or 1 vanilla bean, split lengthwise and seeds scraped)

½ teaspoon (2 mL) cinnamon

5 tablespoons (75 mL) + 1½ teaspoons (7 mL) unsalted butter, divided

2 tablespoons (30 mL) pure maple syrup, more for serving

8 slices fresh pineapple (¼ inch/5 mm thick)

8 slices challah, egg, or sourdough bread (1 inch/ 2.5 cm thick)

1 medium banana, sliced

¾ cup (175 mL) natural coconut chips

Plain full-fat yogurt, for serving (optional)

1. In a medium bowl, whisk together the coconut milk, 2% milk, eggs, vanilla, and cinnamon. Pour the mixture into a 13- × 9-inch (3 L) baking dish.

2. In a large frying pan, melt 2 tablespoons (30 mL) of the butter over medium heat. Once the butter is bubbling, about 1 minute, add the maple syrup and stir with a wooden spoon.

3. Add 4 slices of pineapple at a time to the frying pan and cook for 1 minute. Turn and cook for another minute or until the pineapple slices turn golden brown. Transfer to a plate and cover with foil to keep warm. Repeat with the remaining pineapple slices. Wipe the pan clean.

4. In the same frying pan, heat 2 tablespoons (30 mL) of the butter over medium heat until bubbly, about 1 minute.

5. Meanwhile, place 2 slices of bread in the milk mixture for about 30 seconds per side, pressing down gently so the bread soaks up the custard.

6. Add the soaked bread slices to the frying pan and cook for 1 minute per side, or until lightly golden. Transfer to a baking sheet and cover loosely with foil to keep warm.

7. Working with 2 slices of bread at a time, continue to soak and cook the remaining bread. Add the remaining butter, 1½ teaspoons (7 mL) at a time, each time bread is added to the pan.

8. To serve, place 2 slices of French toast on each plate and top with pineapple, banana, and coconut chips. Top with yogurt and additional maple syrup, as desired.

Coconut Banana Smoothie

Serves 1

I grew up on banana smoothies that my grandmother would make for me when I came home from school. She would serve them with a dash of cinnamon sprinkled on top. Those flavours remind me of my childhood in Santo Domingo and have stayed with me. This is my grown-up version, adding coconut milk and hemp hearts. For this recipe, I use coconut milk from a carton. Canned coconut has a higher fat content and is best used for cooking.

½ cup (125 mL) unsweetened almond milk

½ cup (125 mL) coconut milk (from a carton)

1 tablespoon (15 mL) pure maple syrup

¼ teaspoon (1 mL) pure vanilla extract

½ frozen banana, coarsely chopped

1 tablespoon (15 mL) hemp hearts

1 tablespoon (15 mL) natural peanut butter or almond butter

1 tablespoon (15 mL) unsweetened coconut chips

Cinnamon, for garnish

1. In a high-speed blender, combine the almond milk, coconut milk, maple syrup, vanilla, banana, hemp hearts, and peanut butter. Blend on high speed until smooth and creamy, about 2 minutes.

2. Pour into a glass and top with coconut chips and a sprinkle of cinnamon.

Summer Berry Smoothie

Serves 2

When I lived in Mexico City, after sending my daughters off to school, my morning continued with a run followed by a smoothie. This particular one was the perfect breakfast after a hilly run. Full of antioxidants and healthy fats, this berry smoothie is pure fuel for the body, and since coming back to Canada it is the one I still make after my runs.

1½ cups (375 mL) unsweetened almond milk

1 cup (250 mL) mixed frozen berries (such as raspberries, blueberries, strawberries)

½ frozen banana, coarsely chopped

1 tablespoon (15 mL) raw or roasted cashew butter

½ teaspoon (2 mL) pure almond extract

½ teaspoon (2 mL) chia seeds

½ teaspoon (2 mL) hemp hearts

1. In a high-speed blender, combine the almond milk, frozen berries, banana, cashew butter, almond extract, chia seeds, and hemp hearts. Blend on high speed until smooth and creamy, about 2 minutes.

2. Pour into glasses and serve.

Mexican Hot Chocolate

Serves 3

3 cups (750 mL) whole milk

2 tablespoons (30 mL) crushed cinnamon sticks, broken into large pieces

6 ounces (170 g) semisweet chocolate, finely chopped (I use Valrhona)

3 tablespoons (45 mL) demerara sugar

¾ teaspoon (4 mL) pure almond extract

¼ teaspoon (1 mL) cayenne pepper

Pinch of sea salt

1 teaspoon (5 mL) cornstarch

2 tablespoons (30 mL) water

When we lived in Mexico City, we would take trips to nearby cities and towns on the weekends. One of these was Oaxaca. Known for one of the most beautiful markets in the country, Oaxaca is a culinary gem that has enriched Mexican gastronomy for ages. From the cheese that's used in traditional quesadillas, to its spiced chocolate, memories of this sunny and colourful city come to me often. It was in Oaxaca where I drank the best hot chocolate of my life. Creamy and lightly spiced with cayenne, this nectar of the gods, as it was once called, started our weekend the right way.

During the winter, I like making my own version of Mexican hot chocolate with cinnamon sticks, which I find go so well with the taste of the cayenne. For this recipe, use the best chocolate you can find.

1. In a medium saucepan, combine the milk and cinnamon and simmer over medium-low heat, whisking occasionally, for 10 minutes, or until the cinnamon is fragrant. Make sure the milk does not boil. Strain the milk into a bowl and discard the cinnamon. Pour the milk back into the saucepan.

2. Whisk in the chocolate, demerara sugar, almond extract, cayenne, and salt. Continue to simmer, whisking, until the mixture is smooth and creamy, about 3 minutes.

3. In a small bowl, whisk together the cornstarch and water, then pour into the hot chocolate and simmer, stirring continuously, for 2 minutes.

4. Pour the hot chocolate into mugs and serve while hot.

Melbourne

An unforgettable trip to Sydney, Australia, with daily views of the opera house, Bondi and Manly Beaches, and the harbour, was an introduction to the breathtaking beauty of that country. And the food opened my eyes to the exciting world of modern Australian cuisine, one that's filled with spices, grilled fish, chilies, and extraordinary wines.

I knew I had to return to Australia, and to be precise, I wanted to visit Melbourne, a city that had been on my bucket list for a long time. I had been hearing how Melbourne has an unparalleled coffee scene and how the city's food reflected its diverse multiculturalism—deliciously creative dishes influenced by cultures from all over the world. This is a city that has one of the world's largest Chinatowns and where Greek and Italians that moved there after the gold rush infused the cuisine with ingredients from the Mediterranean. A few years after my first trip to Australia, my partner, Warren, and I went to Melbourne for two weeks to visit friends and to eat our way through this eclectic city.

I soon learned that each neighbourhood in Melbourne takes pride in what makes it different from the others, from the slow-paced, relaxed atmosphere, sunny beaches, and plant-based restaurants of St. Kilda to the busy streets of the central business district where at lunchtime a sea of people stream through the laneways to grab a bowl of pho or a plate of plump dumplings—an ode to the vast South Asian influence in the city.

The city's diversity has resulted in a colourful tapestry of ingredients that have become essential to its cuisine. From chilies and pomegranate molasses to fresh halloumi cheese and lemony sumac, every meal we had during our stay reflected a fusion of cultures.

On any given morning, coffee shops around the city offer variations of luscious avocado toast, always served on tangy sourdough bread and topped with anything from pomegranate seeds and edamame to salmon sashimi to fresh halloumi cheese. The city's coffee is, simply put, the best in the world, smooth and creamy without any need to sweeten it. I happily downed countless cups of flat white, and coffee is one of the reasons why I want to return to Melbourne.

We mainly ate in the Fitzroy neighbourhood, known for its vegetarian restaurants and independent stores. Strolling along Brunswick Street, we had lunch at Transformer, where the dishes seduced us with layer after layer of delectable and exciting flavours that captured the essence of umami. We enjoyed crispy chickpea panisse with truffle salt and smoky cumin-braised eggplant with chermoula, labneh, and mint—a bold combination that made us feel grateful for the chance to visit a city that's a true feast for the senses.

We explored Thai dishes one night, pan-Asian the next, and the most outstanding rustic Mediterranean at Alimentari, where Greek and Italian flavours mingled with Middle Eastern spices. Farro salads dressed with bright green pesto, served with kibbeh wraps, and garlicky eggplant cannelloni filled with silky smooth ricotta, made the perfect feast to end our trip to Melbourne. We felt happy and content with our food adventures in a city that had already started to feel like home.

Lunch

I grew up in a family that to this day eats lunch together. That ignited in me a deep love for real and comforting food, like the dishes made with loving hands by my maternal grandmother. Lunch was filled with laughter, family, and friends dropping by and invited to our table. I remember how my grandfather would come home from a farmers' market nearby with a handful of dried beans or rice, and as we sat at the table for lunch, he would hand me this little gift with the brightest smile. Family lunches for me have always been more than food; they are about togetherness.

In my travels, lunch can take place at a market, surrounded by strangers who feel like family, patiently waiting to taste some of the local cuisine. Lunch can also be a poke bowl on the beach, a slice of pizza in an Italian piazza, or a saucy shakshuka at home.

Chickpea and Feta Salad

Serves 4

1 can (19 ounces/540 mL) chickpeas, drained and rinsed

1 cup (250 mL) cherry tomatoes, cut in half

1 cup (250 mL) crumbled feta cheese

3 green onions (white and light green parts only), chopped

½ cup (125 mL) tightly packed fresh flat-leaf parsley leaves

½ cup (125 mL) tightly packed fresh oregano leaves

1 clove garlic, finely chopped

¼ cup (60 mL) extra-virgin olive oil

¼ cup (60 mL) red wine vinegar

Juice of ½ lemon

Salt and pepper

While spending a day on Aegina, an island just a forty-five-minute ferry ride from Athens, a group of friends and I stopped for lunch in a quaint street in Aegina town. The houses were painted white, with blue and yellow window frames and potted flowers on balconies and next to front doors. We found a little restaurant where we could see fresh fish and octopus being brought in straight from the sea, and we spent a sunny afternoon feasting on grilled calamari, tzatziki, and a lemony chickpea salad that was so simple and fresh that since then, as soon as my summer herbs start to grow, I look forward to making my own version of this memorable salad. Perfect on its own or as a side with Piri-Piri Roasted Fish (page 209).

1. In a medium bowl, combine the chickpeas, cherry tomatoes, feta, green onions, parsley, and oregano.

2. Add the garlic, olive oil, red wine vinegar, and lemon juice. Toss to combine. Season with salt and pepper and serve.

Farro Salad with Pesto, Feta, and Walnuts

Serves 6

2 cups (500 mL) farro

6 cups (1.5 L) water

1 tablespoon (15 mL) sea salt

1½ cups (375 mL) coarsely chopped raw walnuts

1½ cups (375 mL) crumbled feta cheese

1 cup (250 mL) pomegranate seeds

¾ cup (175 mL) Garden Pesto (page 69)

½ cup (125 mL) chopped fresh mint

2 green onions (white and light green parts only), chopped

3 tablespoons (45 mL) fresh lemon juice

2 tablespoons (30 mL) extra-virgin olive oil

½ teaspoon (2 mL) freshly cracked pepper

If you haven't been to Melbourne, Australia, I suggest you put it on your bucket list. Its food scene is one my favourites in the world. This is where different flavours from around the world can easily mingle in one single dish, making it one to remember. It was in the Fitzroy neighbourhood—its streets lined with independent stores, art galleries, and vegetarian restaurants—where I had some of the most delicious salads I've ever eaten.

Inspired by these mouth-watering salads, back home in Canada I made this hearty farro-based salad with feta cheese, fresh pesto, toasted walnuts, and a bit of mint. This salad is delicious on its own, or you can serve it with grilled fish or shrimp on top.

1. Rinse and drain the farro. In a large pot, bring the farro, water, and salt to a boil. Reduce the heat to medium-low and simmer until the farro is just tender, about 35 minutes. Drain any excess water.

2. Meanwhile, in a medium frying pan, toast the walnuts over medium-high heat, stirring often, until fragrant, about 3 minutes.

3. In a large bowl, combine the farro, walnuts, feta, pomegranate seeds, pesto, mint, green onions, lemon juice, olive oil, and pepper. Toss to combine. Enjoy cold or at room temperature. Store in a covered container in the fridge for up to 5 days.

Garden Pesto

Makes 2 cups (500 mL)

3 cups (750 mL) tightly packed
fresh basil leaves

2½ cups (625 mL) tightly
packed fresh flat-leaf parsley
leaves

5 large cloves garlic, coarsely
chopped

1 cup (250 mL) pine nuts,
toasted

½ teaspoon (2 mL) sea salt

½ teaspoon (2 mL) freshly
ground pepper

1¼ cups (300 mL) extra-virgin
olive oil

½ teaspoon (2 mL) lemon zest

2 tablespoons (30 mL) fresh
lemon juice

1 cup (250 mL) finely grated
Parmesan cheese

Whenever I'm in Italy, I go to a market with the sole purpose of bringing back home blocks of Parmigiano-Reggiano cheese to make pesto. In my kitchen this garden pesto isn't just folded into pasta. It is key to my Summer Caprese Salad (page 167), it's folded into Zucchini Pasta with Roasted Salmon and Tomatoes (page 191) or Farro Salad with Pesto, Feta, and Walnuts (page 66), and it's drizzled on Salmon with Shishito Pepper Salad (page 195).

In Florence, where I fell I love with the magic and simplicity of Italian cooking, I once had a bruschetta made with pesto; the tomatoes had been grown nearby, the olive oil was a light shade of green, and the herbs, garlic, and Parmesan fragrantly embraced the chopped tomatoes. Such a simple dish, gloriously elevated by adding just a bit of pesto.

During the summer, my daughter Isabella's dad grows tons of basil and parsley in his garden. I gather baskets full of herbs and make a few batches of pesto that will last several months. This recipe is slightly non-traditional, and the bit of lemon zest and the squeeze of lemon juice make the flavours shine even more.

1. In a food processor, combine the basil, parsley, garlic, pine nuts, salt, and pepper. Blend into a paste.

2. With the motor running, stream in the olive oil and blend for about 10 seconds. Add the lemon zest and juice and blend for 5 seconds.

3. Scrape the pesto into a medium bowl and stir in the Parmesan. Store in a clean jar with a lid or in a covered container in the fridge for up to 2 weeks or in the freezer for up to 4 months. If using from frozen, thaw in the fridge overnight.

Falafel Salad with Tahini Sauce

Serves 6

Tahini Sauce

1 cup (250 mL) tahini

2 cloves garlic, finely minced

1 teaspoon (5 mL) soy sauce

1 teaspoon (5 mL) pure maple syrup

½ teaspoon (2 mL) sea salt

¾ cup (175 mL) boiling water

Falafel Salad

2 cans (19 ounces/540 mL each) chickpeas, drained and rinsed

3 cloves garlic

¾ cup (175 mL) diced Spanish onion

½ cup (125 mL) tightly packed fresh flat-leaf parsley leaves

2 heaping tablespoons (36 mL) all-purpose flour

1 teaspoon (5 mL) ground coriander

1 teaspoon (5 mL) ground cumin

1 teaspoon (5 mL) sea salt

½ teaspoon (2 mL) pepper

Pinch of red chili flakes

4 tablespoons (60 mL) extra-virgin olive oil, divided

When I first moved to Canada to go to university, I lived in Montreal for almost five years. It was the city that opened my eyes to a diversity of cuisines from around the world. It was also the first time I was exposed to so many markets. There was a market near where we lived that had Caribbean produce, and there was the iconic Jean Talon Market, and my favourite, Atwater Market. Living in Montreal meant trying dishes that were new to me and that I soon grew to love. I found a Middle Eastern spot that had some of the best falafels I've ever eaten. Drizzled with tahini sauce and served over tabbouleh, it was my lunch of choice and one that I make at home often even today.

In this recipe, the falafels are baked instead of fried, and they're served over spinach with sweet roasted peppers. They are crispy and deliciously spiced and make a wonderful vegetarian meal.

1. Preheat the oven to 375°F (190°C). Line 2 baking sheets with parchment paper.

2. To make the tahini sauce: In a medium bowl, combine the tahini, garlic, soy sauce, maple syrup, salt, and boiling water. Whisk until smooth. Add a little more water, as needed, if the sauce is too thick. Set aside.

3. To make the falafel mixture: In a food processor, combine the chickpeas, garlic, Spanish onion, parsley, flour, coriander, cumin, salt, pepper, chili flakes, 2 tablespoons (30 mL) of the olive oil, and lemon juice. Pulse until the mixture comes together but is still a bit chunky. You should see small pieces of chickpeas. Transfer the mixture to a large bowl and chill in the fridge for 10 minutes.

4. Meanwhile, place the sweet peppers, skin side up, on a prepared baking sheet and drizzle with 1 tablespoon (15 mL) of the olive oil. Roast for 13 to 15 minutes, or until the skin of the peppers is slightly charred. Set aside, leaving the oven on.

continued

Juice of ½ lemon

2 sweet red peppers, sliced
into wide lengths

1 sweet yellow pepper, sliced
into wide lengths

8 cups (2 L) mixed greens
(such as romaine lettuce,
baby arugula, baby spinach)

1 large English cucumber,
sliced

5. To shape the falafel balls, using about 3 tablespoons (45 mL) of the chickpea mixture at a time, roll between your hands into a ball. If the mixture starts to stick, dust your hands with a little flour. Arrange the falafel balls as they are made on the second prepared baking sheet. Flatten the balls slightly, then drizzle with the remaining 1 tablespoon (15 mL) olive oil. Bake until the falafels are browned and crispy, about 30 minutes, turning the balls halfway through.

6. To serve, arrange the mixed greens on plates. Top with the roasted sweet peppers, cucumber, and falafel balls. Drizzle tahini sauce on top.

Shakshuka

Serves 6

2 tablespoons (30 mL) extra-virgin olive oil

1 tablespoon (15 mL) tomato paste

1 teaspoon (5 mL) harissa paste or powder

½ Spanish onion, finely chopped

1 sweet green pepper, finely chopped

¼ teaspoon (1 mL) sea salt

¼ teaspoon (1 mL) black pepper

2 cloves garlic, finely minced

8 vine-ripened or Roma tomatoes, finely chopped

6 eggs

¼ cup (60 mL) tightly packed chopped fresh flat-leaf parsley leaves, more for serving

½ cup (125 mL) crumbled feta cheese

Labneh or plain full-fat Greek yogurt, for serving

Pita bread, warmed, for serving (optional)

While living in Mexico City, I read Yotam Ottolenghi's cookbook *Jerusalem*, where I discovered shakshuka and knew I had to try it. What's not to love about eggs nestled in a savoury tomato sauce spiced with fiery harissa? I make this at home for my family nearly every Saturday. For my recipe, vine-ripened tomatoes are a must. They are usually sweeter and juicier than Roma tomatoes and have a wonderful flavour when spiced with harissa. The sauce in this shakshuka begs to be topped with tangy dollops of labneh and eaten with warm pita bread.

This is a recipe where fresh herbs make the dish even more flavourful. If you have cilantro on hand, feel free to use it in place of the parsley. For a bit of extra spice, I like to top mine with a few pinches of red chili flakes.

1. In a large frying pan, heat the olive oil over medium heat. Add the tomato paste and cook for 30 seconds, stirring constantly.

2. Add the harissa, Spanish onion, green pepper, salt, and black pepper and cook, stirring often, until the onion is translucent and slightly browned, about 5 minutes. Add the garlic and cook for 30 seconds, stirring constantly.

3. Add the tomatoes, cover with a lid, and reduce the heat to low. Cook for 10 minutes, stirring halfway through.

4. Using a potato masher, mash the tomato mixture. The sauce should be a bit chunky. You want a few pieces of tomato to remain.

5. Break an egg into a small ramekin. Using a spoon, make a small well in the tomato sauce, then gently slip the egg into the well so the egg is coddled in the sauce. Repeat with the remaining 5 eggs. Sprinkle the parsley over the eggs. Cook until the egg whites are set and the yolks are slightly runny, 10 to 12 minutes.

continued

6. Serve in the frying pan, topped with feta and dollops of labneh, with pita bread on the side, if using.

Tip Harissa is a Tunisian hot chili condiment blended with spices such as coriander and saffron. It's widely used in Middle Eastern and North African cuisines and has a wonderful smoky flavour that takes this shakshuka to another level. You can find harissa in the international food aisle at your local grocery store.

Avocado Toast with Beet Hummus

Serves 6

During my stays in Sydney and Melbourne, I quickly lost count of how many avocado toasts I ate. Australia is the birthplace of this worldwide favourite, and I soon discovered that every café takes pride in serving it in their own original way. A poached egg on top is a must for brunch, as well as sashimi salmon or grilled mushrooms. But what about thinly sliced fiery chilies, or pomegranate seeds? You bet. The list goes on and on.

At home, I prefer my avocado toast with dollops of homemade beet hummus, tangy feta cheese, and green onions, while mapping my next Australian visit.

1 medium red beet

1 can (19 ounces/540 mL) chickpeas, drained and rinsed

3 cloves garlic

½ cup (125 mL) tahini

¼ cup (60 mL) tightly packed fresh cilantro leaves, more for serving

¼ cup (60 mL) extra-virgin olive oil

¼ cup (60 mL) water

Juice of 1 lemon

½ teaspoon (2 mL) sea salt

½ teaspoon (2 mL) freshly cracked pepper

6 slices sourdough, rye, or multigrain bread, toasted

2 avocados, pitted, peeled, and sliced

1 cup (250 mL) crumbled feta cheese

2 green onions (white and light green parts only), thinly sliced

3 tablespoons (45 mL) sesame seeds

1. Preheat the oven to 400°F (200°F).

2. Wrap the beet in foil and bake for 40 minutes, or until fork-tender. Remove from the oven, open the foil packet, and let the beet cool. Cut the beet in half.

3. In a food processor or high-speed blender, combine the beet, chickpeas, garlic, tahini, cilantro, olive oil, water, lemon juice, salt, and pepper. Blend on high speed until smooth, scraping down the sides as needed.

4. Top each slice of toast with dollops of beet hummus and avocado slices. Sprinkle with feta, green onions, sesame seeds, and additional cilantro.

Asparagus and Crab Tartine

Serves 4

1 package (8 ounces/225 g)
  lump crab meat, drained

2 tablespoons (30 mL) finely
  chopped fresh chives

2 tablespoons (30 mL) full-fat
  sour cream

Juice of ½ lemon

½ teaspoon (5 mL) curry
  powder

¼ teaspoon (1 mL) sea salt

¼ teaspoon (1 mL) pepper

1 tablespoon (15 mL) extra-
  virgin olive oil

1 tablespoon (15 mL) balsamic
  vinegar

12 asparagus spears, trimmed

4 slices of your favourite
  bread, toasted (I prefer rye
  or sourdough)

2 avocados, pitted, peeled, and
  sliced

1 Thai chili pepper, thinly sliced

I went to San Francisco with the sole purpose of eating my way around the city. First on my list was Tartine Bakery, a mecca for all things bread and pastry. My friend Amy and I arrived with our daughters at eight in the morning and there was already a lineup of people waiting patiently to get in. The smell of croissants and fresh lemon tarts was in the air, and as we got closer to the door our excitement grew more.

Once we were inside, we must have ordered one of everything. Morning buns topped with cinnamon sugar, the flakiest croissants this side of Paris, fruit tarts bursting with berries and vanilla-flecked pastry cream, and of course a tartine. This particular tartine had roasted asparagus, a light béchamel, and Gruyère cheese—totally sublime. Since that trip to San Francisco, tartines have a special place in our home. This recipe calls for crab and avocado—a duo made for summer meals.

1. Preheat the oven to 375°F (190°C). Line a baking sheet with parchment paper.

2. In a medium bowl, combine the crab meat, chives, sour cream, lemon juice, curry powder, salt, and pepper. Set aside.

3. In a small bowl, stir together the olive oil and balsamic vinegar. Arrange the asparagus on the prepared baking sheet and drizzle with the vinaigrette. Bake until fork-tender, 10 to 12 minutes.

4. To serve, top each slice of toast with 3 asparagus spears, 2 heaping tablespoons (36 mL) of the crab mixture, a few slices of avocado, and a few chilies. Season with salt and pepper.

Butternut Squash Frittata

2 cups (500 mL) peeled and cubed butternut squash

3 tablespoons (45 mL) extra-virgin olive oil, divided

½ teaspoon (2 mL) sea salt

½ teaspoon (2 mL) pepper

8 eggs

⅓ cup (75 mL) 2% milk

¾ cup (175 mL) torn fresh mozzarella cheese

½ cup (125 mL) crumbled soft goat cheese

2 green onions (white and light green parts only), thinly sliced

2 tablespoons (30 mL) finely chopped fresh chives

2 tablespoons (30 mL) finely chopped fresh basil

½ cup (125 mL) finely chopped white onion

I love frittatas. In my opinion, their simplicity makes them the perfect meal, whether for breakfast or dinner. And at home it's without a doubt a staple dish that's easily prepared on busy days.

On one of my trips to Venice, I had probably the best frittata of my life. The mozzarella cheese was deliciously fresh, the squash and roasted red pepper had a perfect hint of sweetness, and the spices made it a frittata to remember. At home I love to have this hearty butternut squash frittata baked with fresh herbs, hot from the oven, with a few slices of warm, crusty baguette and a green salad on the side.

1. Preheat the oven to 375°F (190°F). Line a baking sheet with parchment paper.

2. Spread the squash on the prepared baking sheet and toss with 2 tablespoons (30 mL) of the olive oil and a pinch each of salt and pepper. Bake for 18 minutes, or until soft but not mushy.

3. Meanwhile, in a medium bowl, whisk together the eggs, milk, mozzarella cheese, goat cheese, green onions, chives, basil, and salt and pepper to taste until well incorporated.

4. In a medium frying pan, preferably cast iron, heat the remaining 1 tablespoon (15 mL) olive oil over medium heat. Add the white onion and cook, stirring occasionally, until soft and golden brown, about 5 minutes.

5. Add the cooked squash and the egg mixture. Make sure the bottom of the pan is evenly covered in the mixture. Cook, without stirring, for 5 minutes.

6. Transfer to the oven and cook for 15 minutes, setting the oven to broil during the last minute of cooking to slightly brown the top of the frittata. Serve hot or at room temperature.

Halloumi, Sweet Potato, and Eggplant Stack

Serves 4

Vegetarian dishes in Athens are known for having just a few perfect ingredients. On one trip to this ancient city, I went to a café in the middle of the Plaka neighbourhood. After having a fresh pomegranate juice, I ordered a Greek salad and a vegetarian moussaka—layered eggplant in a garlicky tomato sauce spiced with tons of oregano. This incredibly flavourful dish inspired me to develop a recipe where I could layer some of my favourite vegetables and halloumi, which has to be one of my favourite cheeses. With the addition of fresh pesto, this is a dish that vegetarians and non-vegetarians will both rave about.

⅓ cup (75 mL) olive oil

¼ cup (60 mL) balsamic vinegar

1 teaspoon (5 mL) garlic paste

½ teaspoon (2 mL) sea salt

½ teaspoon (2 mL) pepper

2 medium sweet potatoes, sliced into ⅛-inch (3 mm) rounds

1 large Italian eggplant, sliced into ½-inch (1 cm) rounds

2 small zucchini, sliced into ⅛-inch (3 mm) rounds

2 packages (8 ounces/225 g each) halloumi cheese, cut into eight ½-inch (1 cm) slices

⅔ cup (150 mL) Garden Pesto (page 69)

⅓ cup (75 mL) pine nuts, toasted

1. Preheat the oven to 375°F (190°C). Line a baking sheet with parchment paper.

2. In a small bowl, combine the olive oil, balsamic vinegar, garlic paste, salt, and pepper.

3. Place the sweet potatoes on the prepared baking sheet and drizzle with 2 tablespoons (30 mL) of the olive oil mixture. Bake for 5 minutes.

4. Add the eggplant and zucchini, leaving a bit of room between the vegetables so you don't overcrowd the baking sheet. Continue to bake for about 15 minutes, turning the potatoes halfway, until the potatoes are golden brown and fork-tender and the eggplant and zucchini are soft and slightly golden brown.

5. In a large nonstick frying pan over medium-high heat, arrange the slices of halloumi and cook for 1 minute per side, or until golden brown.

6. To assemble, spread 1 tablespoon (15 mL) of the garden pesto in the centre of each plate. Place a slice of sweet potato on top. Spread 1 tablespoon (15 mL) pesto over the sweet potato, followed by a slice of cheese and a slice of eggplant. Spread ½ teaspoon (2 mL) pesto over the eggplant.

7. Top with another slice of cheese, 1 teaspoon (5 mL) garden pesto, and 2 zucchini slices. Sprinkle a few pine nuts on top of each stack and serve while warm.

Spring Quinoa Bowls with Garlic Tahini Sauce

Serves 6

Garlic Tahini Sauce

1 cup (250 mL) tahini

3 cloves garlic, minced

1 teaspoon (5 mL) soy sauce

1 teaspoon (5 mL) pure liquid honey

½ teaspoon (2 mL) sea salt

½ cup (125 mL) boiling water, more as needed for desired consistency

Spring Quinoa Bowls

2 cups (500 mL) white quinoa, rinsed

4 cups (1 L) water

½ teaspoon (2 mL) sea salt

1 tablespoon (15 mL) extra-virgin olive oil or grapeseed oil

1 block (14 ounces/398 g) extra-firm tofu

⅓ cup (75 mL) tamari

3 tablespoons (45 mL) sesame oil

1 can (19 ounces/540 mL) black beans, drained and rinsed

3 medium carrots, peeled and spiralized

3 medium zucchini, spiralized

1½ cups (375 mL) cherry tomatoes, cut in half

3 green onions (white and light green parts only), finely chopped

½ cup (125 mL) coarsely chopped raw walnuts

2 avocados, pitted, peeled, and thinly sliced

¼ cup (60 mL) sesame seeds

My many friends around the world, knowing that as soon as I land, food is the number one thing on my mind, often recommend gems. One such gem was Daluma, a plant-based restaurant in the heart of Berlin's Mitte neighbourhood committed to serving some of the best vegan food I've ever eaten. They are especially known for their grain bowls.

As soon as I returned home I found myself gathering some of my favourite vegetables and topping them with a garlic tahini sauce for this spring quinoa bowl. The bowl is chock full of fresh vegetables, nuts, and golden-brown tofu. Be generous with the garlicky sauce, as it gives this wholesome bowl a punch of flavour.

1. To make the garlic tahini sauce: In a medium bowl, whisk together the tahini, garlic, soy sauce, honey, salt, and boiling water until smooth and creamy. Add a bit more water as needed if the sauce is too thick.

2. To make the spring quinoa bowls: In a medium saucepan, combine the quinoa, water, and salt. Bring to a boil over medium-high heat. Reduce the heat to low, cover with a lid, and simmer for 12 to 14 minutes, until the quinoa is tender and has absorbed all the water. Remove from the heat and fluff with a fork. Set aside, keeping warm.

3. Meanwhile, preheat the oven to 375°F (190°C). Grease a baking sheet with the olive oil.

4. Drain the tofu and pat dry with a kitchen towel. Cut the tofu crosswise into strips ½ inch (1 cm) thick.

5. In a medium bowl, stir together the tamari and sesame oil. Toss the tofu in the mixture to coat and let marinate for 5 minutes.

6. Place the marinated tofu on the baking sheet and bake for 15 minutes, or until golden brown, turning once.

7. To assemble, divide the cooked quinoa among bowls. Top each bowl with 3 or 4 tofu strips, black beans, carrots, zucchini, tomatoes, green onions, walnuts, avocado, and sesame seeds. Top with the garlic tahini sauce and serve.

Chana Masala Bowls

Serves 6

¼ cup (60 mL) coconut oil

1 white onion, finely diced

1 tablespoon + 1½ teaspoons
    (22 mL) ground cumin

1 teaspoon (5 mL) sea salt,
    divided

7 cloves garlic, minced

2 green chilies, sliced

2 tablespoons (30 mL) minced
    fresh ginger

¾ cup (175 mL) loosely packed
    chopped fresh cilantro
    leaves

1 tablespoon (15 mL) ground
    coriander

1½ teaspoons (7 mL) turmeric

1 teaspoon (5 mL) chili powder

1 teaspoon (5 mL) curry
    powder

2 cans (19 ounces/540 mL
    each) chickpeas, drained
    and rinsed

1 can (28 ounces/796 mL)
    puréed or diced tomatoes

2 tablespoons (30 mL)
    coconut sugar

2 tablespoons (30 mL) fresh
    lemon juice

1½ teaspoons (7 mL) garam
    masala

For serving

Cooked basmati rice or
    cauliflower rice

Chopped fresh cilantro leaves

2 avocados, pitted, peeled, and
    sliced

My love of Indian food comes from my dad. An avid traveller, he goes to India often and always comes back raving about dishes he knows I would love. One of these dishes is chana masala.

I find comfort in the flavours of spices like cumin, curry, and garam masala, and if I had to describe the feeling of having a warm bowl of this delicious chickpea-based dish, I would say "food for the soul." Each fall, my dad, my daughters, and I meet up in New York, and on our first night, going out for chana masala is in order. At home, this has become one of our favourite dinners to make, one that my whole family enjoys over piping hot bowls of basmati rice and topped with creamy avocado.

1. In a large pot, melt the coconut oil over medium heat. Add the onion, cumin, and ½ teaspoon (2 mL) of the salt and cook, stirring often, until the onion is soft and translucent, about 5 minutes.

2. Meanwhile, in a food processor, combine the garlic, green chilies, ginger, and cilantro. Pulse for a few seconds, until the mixture is coarsely chopped. Scrape the mixture into the onions and stir to combine.

3. Add the coriander, turmeric, chili powder, and curry powder and stir to coat the onions. Add the chickpeas, tomatoes, and the remaining ½ teaspoon (2 mL) salt. If the mixture is too thick, add up to ½ cup (125 mL) water. You are looking for a semi-thick consistency. Bring to a simmer over medium-high heat, then reduce the heat to medium-low and simmer until the chana masala is thick and stew-like, 18 to 20 minutes.

4. Remove from the heat and stir in the coconut sugar, lemon juice, and garam masala. Enjoy on its own or serve over rice. Top with cilantro and avocado slices.

Vegetable and Manchego Galette

Serves 6

Every trip to Barcelona leads me to La Bouquería Market, the busiest and most lively market in the city, where you can enjoy authentic Catalan gastronomy and buy all kinds of spices (like saffron, a must for paellas), fresh fish, local desserts, and my personal favourite, Manchego cheese. You'll find Manchego on the menu at every tapas bar in Spain.

At home, I love serving it as part of a cheeseboard or in this roasted vegetable galette, where it adds delicious sharpness to the vegetables and flaky pastry.

Pastry

1¼ cups (300 mL) all-purpose flour

¾ teaspoon (4 mL) sea salt

¾ teaspoon (4 mL) freshly ground pepper

½ cup (125 mL/110 g) unsalted butter (1 stick), frozen

⅓ cup (75 mL) ice water, more if needed

2 tablespoons (30 mL) 2% milk

Filling

1 medium sweet potato, peeled and sliced into ⅛-inch (3 mm) rounds

1 small zucchini, sliced

1 cup (250 mL) whole button mushrooms

6 to 8 asparagus spears, trimmed and sliced into 2-inch (5 cm) pieces

½ cup (125 mL) sliced sweet red peppers

½ medium red onion, thinly sliced

1 tablespoon (15 mL) extra-virgin olive oil

1. To make the pastry: In a large bowl, whisk together the flour, salt, and pepper. Using the large holes of a box grater, grate the butter over the flour mixture. Gently toss the grated butter into the flour mixture to evenly distribute it.

2. Stir in the ice water with a fork until the mixture is evenly moistened. If the dough feels dry, add 1 to 2 teaspoons (5 to 10 mL) more ice water and stir until combined.

3. Scrape the dough onto a work surface and knead gently until the dough comes together, about 2 minutes. Shape the dough into a disc ¼ inch (5 mm) thick. Wrap in plastic wrap and refrigerate for at least 1 hour.

4. Position a rack in the middle of the oven. Preheat the oven to 450°F (230°C). Line a baking sheet with parchment paper.

5. To make the filling: In a medium saucepan, cover the sweet potatoes with an inch or so of cold water. Bring to a boil, then reduce the heat and simmer the potatoes for 5 minutes, or until just tender. Drain the potatoes.

6. In a large bowl, stir the potatoes, zucchini, mushrooms, asparagus, red pepper, red onion, olive oil, thyme, pepper, and salt and toss to combine.

7. Using a lightly floured rolling pin, roll out the pastry on a lightly floured work surface into a 14-inch (35 cm) circle. Carefully lift the pastry by gently sliding a thin metal spatula underneath it and transfer it to the prepared baking sheet.

continued

½ teaspoon (2 mL) fresh
    thyme leaves

½ teaspoon (2 mL) freshly
    ground pepper

¼ teaspoon (1 mL) sea salt

½ cup (125 mL) full-fat sour
    cream

3 tablespoons (45 mL) finely
    grated Parmesan cheese

3 tablespoons (45 mL) grated
    Manchego cheese

6 small vine-ripened tomatoes
    on the stem

8. In a small bowl, stir together the sour cream, Parmesan, and Manchego cheese. Spread the sour cream mixture evenly over the dough, leaving a 1½-inch (4 cm) border. Scatter the vegetables evenly over top. Fold the pastry border up over the filling, pleating where needed. Top the filling with the vine of tomatoes.

9. Lightly brush the pastry border with a little milk, being careful not to let any milk get under the dough. Bake until the pastry is light golden brown and the vegetables are fork-tender, 25 to 28 minutes.

10. Place the baking sheet on a rack and let cool slightly. Serve warm or at room temperature.

Tip Manchego cheese is delicious on its own, but when added to sauces it elevates the flavour, adding a nutty, tangy, and slightly sweet taste. You can find Manchego cheese in the specialty cheese section of your grocery store.

Sesame Noodles with Maple-Harissa Tofu Steaks

Serves 4

1 block (12 ounces/350 g)
  extra-firm tofu

2 tablespoons (30 mL)
  extra-virgin olive oil

1 tablespoon + 2 teaspoons
  (25 mL) pure maple syrup

1½ teaspoons (7 mL) harissa
  paste

¼ teaspoon (1 mL) sea salt

1 clove garlic, finely chopped

1 tablespoon + 1½ teaspoons
  (22 mL) cornstarch

1 pound (450 g) whole wheat
  spaghettini or soba noodles

⅓ cup (75 mL) sesame oil

¼ cup (60 mL) soy sauce

½ teaspoon (2 mL) grated
  fresh ginger

2 green onions (white and
  light green parts only),
  chopped

For serving

½ cup (125 mL) raw peanuts,
  lightly crushed

Fresh cilantro leaves

½ sweet red pepper, thinly
  sliced

½ sweet orange pepper, thinly
  sliced

2 tablespoons (30 mL) sesame
  seeds (optional)

Barcelona is one of my favourite cities. Not only do you find some of the best Spanish food there, but the city is filled with restaurants showcasing the cuisines of countries as diverse as Italy, Japan, and, because it's close by, Morocco.

I remember having a vegetarian dish with harissa, a hot chili paste made with garlic, spices such as coriander and caraway, and olive oil. The flavour of the harissa paste was the key ingredient to the pasta and roasted vegetables I had, so as soon as we finished lunch, I stopped at a nearby market and bought a jar to bring home. Experimenting with flavours is what I love to do the most in my kitchen, and that's how this recipe was born. It mixes sweet and savoury and adds that incomparable taste and a kick of fresh ginger.

1. Preheat the oven to 375°F (190°C). Lightly oil a baking sheet.

2. Drain the tofu and pat dry with a kitchen towel. Cut the tofu crosswise into strips ½ inch (1 cm) thick.

3. In a medium bowl, combine the olive oil, maple syrup, harissa paste, salt, and garlic. Stir until smooth. Place the tofu in a large shallow dish and cover with the maple harissa marinade. Let marinate for 10 minutes.

4. Drain the tofu, discarding the marinade, and transfer to the prepared baking sheet. Sprinkle the cornstarch evenly over the tofu slices. Bake for 15 minutes, or until golden brown, turning once.

5. Meanwhile, boil the spaghettini in a large pot of salted water until just tender. Drain the pasta and rinse under cold running water until the pasta is cool. Return the pasta to the pot.

6. In a medium bowl, stir together the sesame oil, soy sauce, ginger, and green onions.

7. Add the baked tofu to the pot with the pasta. Add the sesame oil mixture and mix with tongs until the pasta is well coated.

8. To serve, divide the tofu pasta mixture among bowls and top with peanuts, cilantro, sliced sweet peppers, and sesame seeds, if using.

Roasted Cauliflower and Romesco Tostadas

Serves 8

Romesco Sauce

1 jar (12 ounces/340 g) roasted red peppers, drained

3 Roma tomatoes, chopped

2 cloves garlic

1 cup (250 mL) slivered raw almonds

¼ cup (60 mL) tightly packed fresh flat-leaf parsley leaves, more for serving

2 tablespoons (30 mL) extra-virgin olive oil

1 tablespoon (15 mL) sherry vinegar

Juice of ½ lemon

½ teaspoon (2 mL) sea salt

½ teaspoon (2 mL) freshly cracked pepper

Tostadas

1 large head cauliflower, cut into small florets

¼ cup (60 mL) extra-virgin olive oil

1 tablespoon (15 mL) balsamic vinegar

1 tablespoon (15 mL) sweet paprika

½ teaspoon (2 mL) sea salt

½ teaspoon (2 mL) pepper

½ cup (125 mL) raw pepitas

8 corn tostadas

¾ cup (175 mL) crumbled feta cheese

4 green onions (white and light green parts only), chopped

The first time I tried romesco I was spending an afternoon in La Barceloneta, Barcelona's beach neighbourhood. It came as a dip with *patatas bravas* (a roasted potato tapas dish that's usually served with a lightly spicy tomato aïoli) and it was absolutely glorious. This delicious red pepper and almond sauce is originally from Tarragona, in Catalonia, and the fishermen in the area made it to be eaten with fish. Romesco can be found on menus across Spain and for all the right reasons. It adds a layer of flavour to any dish, such as these cauliflower tostadas, a hearty and nutritious vegetarian dish that will also be a hit with meat eaters.

1. To make the romesco sauce: In a high-speed blender, combine the red peppers, tomatoes, garlic, almonds, parsley, olive oil, sherry vinegar, lemon juice, salt, and pepper. Pulse until smooth. Set aside.

2. To make the tostadas: Preheat the oven to 375°F (190°C). Line a baking sheet with parchment paper.

3. In a medium bowl, toss together the cauliflower florets, olive oil, balsamic vinegar, paprika, salt, and pepper. Spread evenly on the prepared baking sheet and roast until golden brown, about 20 minutes, stirring halfway through.

4. Meanwhile, in a medium frying pan, toast the pepitas, stirring constantly, until fragrant, about 3 minutes.

5. To assemble, spread about 2 tablespoons (30 mL) of the romesco sauce over each tostada. Top with roasted cauliflower, feta, pepitas, and green onions. Serve immediately.

Tip Tostadas are corn tortillas that are deep-fried or toasted. You can find them in the international food aisle in the grocery store.

Wild Mushroom Quesadillas

Serves 4

Quesadillas are the quintessential Mexican snack. While living in Mexico City, we would have them almost every day. They are so simple to prepare: sandwich cheese and vegetables in a corn tortilla and heat it until the cheese melts and the tortillas are nice and golden. These mushroom quesadillas are hearty, garlicky, and perfect for a quick lunch. We make them at home to have with soups when we want a more substantial meal.

2 tablespoons (30 mL) extra-virgin olive oil

2 cloves garlic, finely chopped

1 pound (450 g) mixed mushrooms (such as shiitake, oyster, enoki, cremini), stems removed and coarsely chopped

¼ teaspoon (1 mL) sea salt

¼ teaspoon (1 mL) pepper

¼ cup (60 mL) tightly packed fresh flat-leaf parsley leaves

8 corn tortillas

8 ounces (225 g) fresh mozzarella cheese, torn in small pieces

½ cup (125 mL) of your favourite salsa or Mexican hot sauce, for serving (I like Valentina hot sauce)

1. In a medium frying pan, heat the olive oil over medium heat. Add the garlic and cook for 30 seconds, stirring often so it does not burn.

2. Add the mushrooms, salt, and pepper. Cook for 5 minutes, until the mushrooms have reduced a bit in size. Stir in the parsley, then scrape the mixture into a medium bowl.

3. Wipe the pan clean and return to medium heat. Toast the corn tortillas, one at a time, for 1 minute per side.

4. Place a few pieces of cheese over just half of each tortilla and scatter about 2 tablespoons (30 mL) of the mushroom mixture over the cheese. Fold the other half of the tortilla over the filling.

5. Heat the same pan over medium heat. Add the quesadillas and cook for 1 minute per side, until the tortillas are lightly charred and the cheese is melted. Serve hot with your favourite salsa on the side.

Roasted Eggplant Tacos

Serves 4

Visiting the town of Puebla, Mexico, led me to discover that tacos, the essential Mexican street food, also have roots in Lebanon. Puebla has a big Lebanese community, and the flavours of the Middle East infuse grilled meats and vegetables to create mouth-watering combinations that are cradled in fragrant and smoky corn tortillas. These roasted eggplant tacos are spiced with lemony sumac and za'atar and topped with luscious labneh and fresh tomato salsa. Who said vegetarian tacos were boring?

Salsa

1 cup (250 mL) cherry tomatoes, cut in half

3 green onions (green part only), cut in half crosswise

2 tablespoons (30 mL) minced fresh chives

2 tablespoons (30 mL) drained capers

1 tablespoon (15 mL) extra-virgin olive oil

Juice of 1 lime

Salt and pepper

Roasted Eggplant Tacos

1 pound (450 g) Chinese eggplant, cut into 2-inch (5 cm) cubes

1 teaspoon (5 mL) sea salt, divided

1 tablespoon + 1½ teaspoons (22 mL) sesame oil

½ teaspoon (2 mL) za'atar

½ teaspoon (2 mL) sumac

8 corn tortillas

¾ cup (175 mL) labneh or plain full-fat Greek yogurt

1 cup (250 mL) tightly packed fresh cilantro leaves

¾ cup (175 mL) tomatillo sauce (optional)

1. To make the salsa: In a medium bowl, combine the tomatoes, green onions, chives, capers, olive oil, lime juice, and salt and pepper to taste. Mix well.

2. Preheat the oven to 375°F (190°C).

3. To make the eggplant tacos: Place the eggplant in a colander set over a large bowl or in the sink. Sprinkle with ½ teaspoon (2 mL) of the salt. Let sit for 10 minutes to draw out any bitterness from the eggplant. Rinse the eggplant and pat dry with paper towels.

4. Arrange the eggplant on a baking sheet. Drizzle with the sesame oil, then sprinkle with the za'atar, sumac, and remaining ½ teaspoon (2 mL) salt. Roast until golden and crispy, stirring halfway through, about 12 minutes.

5. Meanwhile, in a large frying pan over medium-high heat, lightly toast the corn tortillas, one at a time, for about 1 minute per side.

6. To assemble, spread about 1 tablespoon (15 mL) labneh over each tortilla. Scatter a few pieces of roasted eggplant on top along with 1 to 2 tablespoons (15 to 30 mL) of the salsa and cilantro. Drizzle 1 to 2 tablespoons (15 to 30 mL) tomatillo sauce on top, if using.

Tip Tomatillo sauce is a deliciously flavourful Mexican salsa made with green tomatillos, garlic, and chilies. You can find it in the international food aisle in the grocery store.

Salmon Tacos with Chipotle Crema

Serves 4

Salmon Tacos

1 skinless wild salmon fillet
    (1¼ pounds/565 g)

¼ cup (60 mL) fresh lime juice

2 tablespoons (30 mL)
    extra-virgin olive oil

2 cloves garlic, finely chopped

½ teaspoon (2 mL) chipotle
    chili powder

½ teaspoon (2 mL) sea salt

8 corn tortillas

2 cups (500 mL) finely
    shredded purple cabbage

3 green onions (white and
    light green parts only),
    thinly sliced

2 avocados, pitted, peeled, and
    sliced

1½ cups (375 mL) crumbled
    feta cheese

¾ cup (175 mL) tightly packed
    fresh cilantro leaves

Chipotle Crema

¾ cup (175 mL) full-fat sour
    cream

3 tablespoons (45 mL) adobo
    sauce (from a 7-ounce/200 g
    can of chipotle peppers in
    adobo sauce)

1 tablespoon (15 mL) fresh lime
    juice

Years of living in Mexico City left me with a passion for regional Mexican cuisine. Spices and dried peppers are ground to create fiery dishes that are simple yet full of flavourful layers that are deliciously satisfying.

The foundation of every taco is a corn tortilla. These are usually made daily and can be found in every market across the city. Sauces and local cheeses are added, and the freshest guacamole tops these tasty delicacies. At home in Canada, salmon tacos are a summer staple that we love to top with a lightly spicy chipotle crema and a good squeeze of lemon. For this recipe, use only the adobo sauce. Store the chipotle peppers in the fridge to add to creamy soups for a bit of spice.

1. Preheat the oven to 375°F (190°C).

2. To make the salmon tacos: Place the salmon in a medium baking dish. In a small bowl, whisk together the lime juice, olive oil, garlic, chili powder, and salt. Pour over the salmon and let marinate at room temperature for 15 minutes.

3. Meanwhile, make the chipotle crema: In a medium bowl, stir together the sour cream, adobo sauce (without the peppers), and lime juice.

4. Bake the salmon for 25 minutes, setting the oven to broil for the last 2 minutes. This will create a nice golden-brown crust. Cut the salmon into 8 equal portions.

5. In a medium frying pan over medium-high heat, lightly toast the corn tortillas, one at a time, for 1 minute per side.

6. To assemble, spread a generous spoonful of chipotle crema over each tortilla. Top with a portion of salmon, cabbage, green onions, avocado, feta, and cilantro.

Peruvian Ceviche with a Twist

Serves 6

Peru is a country with one of the most vibrant cuisines in South America, built on centuries of tradition while incorporating the flavours newcomers brought during the 1900s. There are countless varieties of potatoes and corn, ingredients that are a feature of Peruvian gastronomy. Seafood, from grilled fish to ceviche, can be found in many restaurants and cafés, especially in Lima. Ceviche is a dish of raw fish that gets "cooked" in lime juice, peppers, and onions. In Lima, a slice of sweet potato is often added.

This recipe is inspired not only by the ceviche I had while visiting Lima but by my stepfather, an avid home cook. One of his favourite things to make is ceviche, and it's one of the first things he makes for me when I'm back in Dominican Republic.

1 large sweet potato

1½ pounds (675 g) skinless white fish fillets (such as tilapia, halibut, haddock)

½ large red onion, thinly sliced

1 sweet red pepper, thinly sliced

2 cloves garlic, thinly sliced

½ cup (125 mL) tightly packed fresh flat-leaf parsley leaves

½ teaspoon (2 mL) sea salt

½ teaspoon (2 mL) freshly cracked pepper

1 cup (250 mL) fresh lime juice (about 8 limes)

1 tablespoon (15 mL) extra-virgin olive oil

1 Thai chili pepper, thinly sliced (optional)

1. Peel the sweet potato and cut it in half lengthwise. Then cut the halves into ½-inch (1 cm) slices.

2. Transfer the sweet potatoes to a large saucepan. Cover with an inch or so of water and bring to a simmer over medium-high heat. Reduce the heat and simmer the potatoes until fork-tender, about 12 minutes. Drain the potatoes.

3. Chop the fish into 1-inch (2.5 cm) cubes and place in a large bowl. Add the sweet potatoes, red onion, red pepper, garlic, parsley, salt, black pepper, lime juice, olive oil, and chili pepper, if using. Toss to coat. Let marinate in the fridge until the fish begins to turn opaque, about 30 minutes.

4. Enjoy cold, on its own. Store in a covered container in the fridge for up to 3 days.

Hawaiian Poke Bowls

Serves 2

¾ pound (340 g) sushi-grade
tuna, cut into ½-inch (1 cm)
cubes

⅓ cup (75 mL) soy sauce

⅓ cup (75 mL) toasted sesame
oil

½ teaspoon (2 mL) red chili
flakes

1½ cups (375 mL) sushi rice

3 cups (750 mL) water

½ teaspoon (2 mL) sea salt

½ medium red onion, thinly
sliced

⅓ cup (75 mL) unseasoned rice
vinegar

½ cup (125 mL) chopped green
onions (green part only)

½ English cucumber, thinly
sliced

2 teaspoons (10 mL) pickled
ginger

2 tablespoons (30 mL) sesame
seeds

1 avocado, pitted, peeled, and
sliced

½ cup (125 mL) tightly packed
fresh cilantro leaves

I first tried poke in Hawaii, and I still remember how it opened a whole new world of flavours for me. Maybe it was how the sesame oil and soy sauce flavoured the fresh ahi tuna, or how simple ingredients like rice and avocado complemented this dish so well. I must have eaten poke every day during my visit. It is one of the most emblematic dishes in Waikiki, and you will find it everywhere throughout the island, from restaurants and food trucks to taco joints and local delis. At home, I often make poke during the summer months and always marinate my tuna in toasted sesame oil paired with soy sauce, which gives it a rich, deep, nutty flavour.

1. Place the tuna in a medium bowl. Add the soy sauce, sesame oil, and chili flakes and toss to coat. Let marinate in the fridge for 15 to 20 minutes.

2. Meanwhile, cook the sushi rice. Combine the rice and water. Add the salt to the water. Bring to a boil. Stir, cover, and simmer over low heat for 12 minutes, or until the water is absorbed. Set aside.

3. Meanwhile, in a small bowl, toss the red onions with the rice vinegar. Let marinate until ready to serve the poke bowl.

4. Divide the rice between medium bowls. Top with the marinated tuna, discarding the marinade. Top each bowl with the drained red onions, green onions, cucumber, pickled ginger, sesame seeds, avocado, and cilantro.

Blackened Fish over Yuca Fries

Serves 2

Growing up in Dominican Republic meant that on the weekends my family would go to the beach. Usually lunch would be blackened fish with yuca fries. Garlicky, crispy, and so tasty! Since then, this simple yet utterly delicious meal always brings back memories of those carefree days spent on the beach with my family. Today, that same crispy blackened fish, seasoned with garlic and oregano, is a staple in our home in Canada. The marinade infuses the fish with a zesty flavour, and once the fish is served with fried onions and crispy yuca fries, then you are in for a true taste of a Dominican classic.

2 skinless tilapia fillets
(6 ounces/170 g each)

6 tablespoons (90 mL)
extra-virgin olive oil, divided

Juice of 1 lime

½ teaspoon (2 mL) dried
oregano

1 teaspoon (5 mL) ground
coriander

1 teaspoon (5 mL) sweet
paprika

1 teaspoon (5 mL) sea salt,
divided

1 teaspoon (5 mL) pepper,
divided

1 large yuca root

½ red onion, thinly sliced

1 clove garlic, finely minced

½ lemon

1 avocado, pitted, peeled, and
thinly sliced

1 cup (250 mL) loosely packed
microgreens

1. Preheat the oven to 375°F (190°C). Line a baking sheet with parchment paper.

2. Place the fish fillets in a shallow baking dish. In a small bowl, combine 2 tablespoons (30 mL) of the olive oil, lime juice, oregano, coriander, paprika, ½ teaspoon (2 mL) of the salt, and ½ teaspoon (2 mL) of the pepper. Whisk until blended. Pour over the fillets and let marinate at room temperature for 10 minutes.

3. Meanwhile, bring a medium pot of water to a boil. While you're waiting for the water to boil, peel the yuca, cut it in half lengthwise, then cut each half into thick wedges. Boil the yuca until the wedges are slightly soft (test with a fork), about 6 minutes. Drain the yuca wedges and transfer them to the prepared baking sheet.

4. Toss the yuca wedges with 2 tablespoons (30 mL) of the olive oil and the remaining ½ teaspoon (2 mL) salt and ½ teaspoon (2 mL) pepper. Spread in a single layer, leaving a bit of space between the wedges, and bake until crispy and golden, about 20 minutes, turning halfway through.

5. Meanwhile, in a medium frying pan, heat 1 tablespoon (15 mL) of the olive oil over medium-high heat. Place the fillets in the pan (discarding the marinade) and cook until golden brown and crispy, about 5 minutes per side. Transfer to a plate and cover loosely with foil to keep warm.

continued

6. In a small frying pan, heat the remaining 1 tablespoon (15 mL) olive oil over medium heat. Add the onions and fry until soft and translucent, about 5 minutes. Add the garlic and cook, stirring constantly, for 30 seconds. Remove from the heat.

7. To serve, place a fillet on each plate, and add yuca fries and fried onions on the side. Squeeze lemon juice over the fish and fried onions. Enjoy with a few slices of avocado and microgreens on the side.

Tip Yuca is the root of the cassava plant. It has a rough bark-like skin that must be peeled before cooking. Once cooked, its texture is similar to that of potatoes, and it has a mildly sweet flavour. It's also delicious when mashed. You can find it in the produce section of most grocery stores.

Manly Beach Salmon Burgers

Makes 8 burgers

2 pounds (900 g) skinless wild salmon fillets, chopped into 2- to 3-inch (5 to 8 cm) pieces

½ medium Spanish onion, chopped

2 cloves garlic

2 green onions (white and light green parts only), chopped

½ cup (125 mL) tightly packed chopped fresh cilantro leaves

½ teaspoon (2 mL) minced fresh ginger

1 teaspoon (5 mL) Dijon mustard

1 teaspoon (5 mL) soy sauce

1½ teaspoons (7 mL) sea salt, divided

1 teaspoon (5 mL) black pepper

½ teaspoon (2 mL) sweet paprika

2 cups (500 mL) panko crumbs, divided

½ sweet red pepper

½ sweet orange pepper

½ sweet yellow pepper

2 tablespoons (30 mL) extra-virgin olive oil

I once spent a few days in Manly, a beach town not far from Sydney, Australia, and I fell in love with its breathtaking beaches, white sand, active lifestyle, and fantastic food. My mornings would start with an acai bowl, then a long run along the beach, followed by a ferry ride into Sydney to spend the day with friends. I would come back to Manly later in the evening and have dinner at the same restaurant facing the beach. On the menu was a salmon burger seasoned with ginger, lemongrass, and soy. Coated in a little panko, the burger was crispy on the outside and juicy and tender on the inside. It was the perfect meal to end a day spent walking the streets of Sydney and marvelling at its out-of-this-world food scene. At home, I love making my version of these burgers in the summer and topping them with sweet roasted peppers and creamy avocado for a true taste of summer in Australia.

1. Preheat the oven to 375°F (190°C). Line 2 baking sheets with parchment paper.

2. In a food processor, combine the salmon, onion, garlic, green onions, cilantro, ginger, mustard, soy sauce, 1 teaspoon (5 mL) of the salt, black pepper, and paprika. Pulse until the mixture is slightly chunky. Scrape the mixture into a large bowl and stir in ½ cup (125 mL) of the panko.

3. Scoop about ½ cup (125 mL) of the mixture per burger and shape into 8 patties about ½ inch (1 cm) thick. Arrange the patties on a prepared baking sheet and freeze for 15 minutes. This will help them keep their shape when being coated in panko.

4. Meanwhile, cut the sweet peppers into strips ½ inch (1 cm) wide. Spread them on the other prepared baking sheet and drizzle with the olive oil and balsamic vinegar. Roast until slightly charred, about 15 minutes, turning halfway through. Transfer the peppers to a plate and cover with foil to keep warm.

continued

2 tablespoons (30 mL)
  balsamic vinegar
1 cup (250 mL) full-fat sour
  cream
¼ cup (60 mL) finely minced
  fresh chives
8 brioche burger buns
8 leaves romaine lettuce
2 avocados, peeled, pitted, and
  sliced

5. In a shallow baking dish, spread the remaining 1½ cups (375 mL) panko. Coat both sides of each patty with the panko, gently shaking off any excess crumbs. Return the patties to the baking sheet. Bake until the burgers are crispy and golden brown, about 20 minutes, turning them halfway through.

6. Meanwhile, in a medium bowl, stir together the sour cream, chives, and the remaining ½ teaspoon (2 mL) salt.

7. Spread the sour cream mixture on each half of the burger buns. Place a burger on each bottom half and top with roasted peppers, lettuce, avocado, and the top half of the bun.

Tip The uncooked salmon burgers freeze well, and having a few extra is a time saver on busy days. Freeze in an airtight container, separating each burger with wax paper, for up to 1 month.

Florence

I embarked on a train to Florence on an early-summer's day. My friend Tyler and I had arrived in Venice the night before and sleepily made our way to the train station while sipping espressos and making plans for our stay. As soon as we arrived in Florence, we left our bags at the studio we had rented and went out to explore the cradle of the Renaissance—a city I had been wanting to visit since studying art history in my early twenties.

Tyler and I decided to grab a quick bite to eat before setting out for some sightseeing. Friends had told me that Florence was full of gastronomic delights, with delicious street fare such as panini, gelato shops at every turn, and trattorias and cafés that made the city a food lover's heaven. We stopped at La Ménagère, a beautifully designed concept store inside a former household products store—the first to open in Florence, in the 1800s. La Ménagère recreates the mood of an old-school Florentine trattoria, as well as being home to a local flower shop and a small café. We started our day with foamy cappuccinos and croissants. Before we knew it, it was time for lunch, so we went to the restaurant located in the adjacent light-filled room. On the menu that day, house-made gnocchi, lightly pan-fried in a fragrant sage butter, were light and tender. A side of grilled octopus completed our first meal in Florence and made the perfect start to our adventures in the city.

We walked a few streets over and my heart skipped a beat at my first glimpse of the iconic Duomo, the thirteenth-century Cattedrale di Santa Maria del Fiore. I took in the breathtaking sight and started taking countless pictures, wanting to capture this magnificent work of architecture. Little did I know that the images of that day still live in my memory as if it was yesterday.

On our way to the San Lorenzo market, we walked by a few piazzas where children played and fruit vendors chatted with families. At the main market we learned that it had been built when Florence was still the capital of Italy, around 1870. The ground floor is filled with stalls where vendors sell local cheeses, fruits and vegetables, meats and fish of all kinds, a vast selection of dried mushrooms and sun-dried tomatoes, and the most delicate truffle oil and honeys. I picked up a bag of dried porcini mushrooms and a local cheese with truffles before going up to the second floor, where a gourmet food court offers a wide variety of Tuscan specialties.

We ended our day at a nearby piazza, enjoying a light dinner of a board of local cheeses with warm elderflower honey. As we drizzled the honey over the cheese and took in the view around us, I felt overwhelmingly lucky to be able to experience moments like these, wandering the streets of some of the most beautiful cities, while visiting its markets and eating local delicacies.

Before leaving the piazza we had a simple bruschetta. The tomatoes were ripe and juicy and infused with freshly picked basil and local fruity olive oil. Right there and then, I understood that Italian cuisine is unapologetically simple, but it is the freshness of each ingredient that makes it one of the best in the world. It is food made for the heart.

Barcelona

Barcelona is a city of neighbourhoods, each with its own identity and flair, and it instantly became my favourite place in the world. During a three-day stay one spring, this fantastic city made its way into my heart and my taste buds.

Barcelona's food scene is one of the most vibrant in the world, where recipes that are centuries old mingle with innovative ones carefully created by some of the top chefs in the city. Like most regions in Spain, Catalonia has its own rich history and distinctive culture, which translates into a distinctive cuisine with influences from France and Italy. Catalan cuisine is truly Mediterranean and based on produce from both the land and the sea.

Every time I visit Barcelona, I like to start my day going for a walk around the magical streets of the Barri Gòtic, or the Gothic Quarter, where a labyrinth of medieval alleyways tells the story of how this magnificent city was created. I stop for a coffee at Nomad before making my way to Plaza Real to admire the beauty of the pale yellow buildings that surround this breathtaking and vibrant square. People sit at one of the many restaurants that surround the square to enjoy piping hot plates of paella or fish stew for tapas while sipping sangria. The plaza is always busy, but on Sundays there's a slower pace, and older men set up little tables covered with old coins, books, maps, cards, and stamps and trade them with heartwarming camaraderie.

From Plaza Real, I take a short walk to La Rambla, a tree-lined semi-pedestrian street that forms the boundary between the Gothic Quarter to the east and the colourful and picturesque El Raval neighbourhood to the west. Less than a block away is the magnificent Boquería Market, where I wander among all the spice, fruit, and cheese stalls, picking bright green olive oil made with Arbequina olives, saffron threads to flavour soups and seafood paella, and a few wedges of Manchego cheese to enjoy with plump local figs. Every visit to the market is filled with flavours, aromas, colours, and the buzz of one of Europe's oldest and most iconic food markets, where most of the vendors have been there for generations. Before leaving, I stop by El Quim de la Boquería, a restaurant inside the market that makes traditional Catalan food. It's a seafood paradise, where diners from all over the world line up to feast on such dishes as fresh anchovies lightly bathed in olive oil and vinegar or grilled squid, followed by the house special of fried eggs and chipirones—baby squid—while sipping local draft beer or chilled cava. I go for the cava, and I leave the market with a bag full of treasures to cook in my kitchen.

The pace of the city during the summertime is relaxed and unhurried. All roads seem to lead to the Barceloneta, with its sandy beaches and pristine, deep turquoise waters, and where I head to soak up the sun—but also to enjoy mussels in a garlicky tomato and white wine broth from one of the many chiringuitos, or beachside restaurants.

Dinnertime, as in many European cities, doesn't start until late, usually after nine. That gives me time to go for a walk in my favourite neighbourhood in the city. El Born is a charming maze of narrow streets lined with pale terracotta-coloured buildings. Each apartment faces the street, their balconies filled with lush plants and colourful flowers. The streets are usually busy with people going in and out of the many tapas bars and independent stores, and you will find large groups of friends and family gathered at one of the neighbourhood's plazas catching up over drinks. This makes El Born one of the most eclectic spots in the city.

Just before going for dinner, I stop at El Xampanyet, a tiny bar just around the corner from the Picasso Museum. El Xampanyet is a temple to sparkling wine and excellent food that dates back to 1929. Don't be surprised if you come for half an hour and end up staying for three, while feasting on traditional *tortilla de patatas*, a dish made with only lightly beaten eggs and slowly cooked onions and potatoes. Dinner is usually a two-hour event—or longer if you're out with a large group of friends—where you might be treated to a variety of luscious oysters that taste of the ocean, Manchego cheese with crunchy Marcona almonds, and my personal favourite, lobster or shrimp croquettes—plump pieces of seafood folded into a thick and creamy béchamel sauce, rolled into balls, and fried until crispy and golden brown. Main courses might feature Catalan sausage or tender cod, and grilled octopus is a must, especially the Galician octopus specialty that comes with thinly sliced potatoes lightly covered in olive oil and local smoked paprika. Don't leave the city without trying *fideuá en tinta de calamar*, a dish similar to paella but made with short noodles and a squid-ink base.

I like to finish my meal with crema catalana and smile like a child every time the caramelized sugar on top crackles when my spoon first hits it.

Soups, Starters, and Salads

Some days, regardless of the country I'm in, all I want for lunch or dinner is a bowl of soup and a fresh salad. In Barcelona, a bowl of gazpacho is always in order. In Italy, cioppino. And if I'm visiting my family in Dominican Republic, pumpkin soup with slices of local avocado and a handful of fresh cilantro on top. At home, we live on soups through the winter. From curried lentil soup to fiery bowls of chana masala, there's nothing more comforting than a piping hot pot of soup shared with family. We usually make crostini or quesadillas to go with it and make it a weeknight meal.

Though I make side salads for lunch and dinner year-round, it is during the summer that salads become the main dish in my home. Caprese salad is a favourite dinner of my family, as is any salad with halloumi cheese on it, like my Watermelon, Strawberry, Mint, and Halloumi Salad (page 156). If you are looking for a more substantial starter before your meal, or something to share with a group of friends, try the Baked Feta with Spicy Tomato Sauce (page 139) or Eggplant Escabeche (page 135).

Dominican Pumpkin Soup

Serves 4

6 cups (1.5 L) vegetable stock

6 cups (1.5 L) peeled and cubed pumpkin or butternut squash

2 tablespoons (30 mL) extra-virgin olive oil

1½ Spanish onions, chopped

5 green onions (white and light green parts only), chopped

4 cloves garlic, finely minced

1½ cups (375 mL) tightly packed fresh cilantro leaves, divided, more for serving

1 teaspoon (5 mL) sea salt

1 teaspoon (5 mL) freshly ground pepper

½ cup (125 mL) finely grated Parmesan cheese, more for serving

½ cup (125 mL) raw pepitas, toasted

If I had to choose my favourite Dominican dish, it would be, without a doubt, Dominican pumpkin soup. Especially if made by my mother! In Santo Domingo, soups are made whenever it's rainy and the temperature drops a bit. What makes this soup different from any other pumpkin or butternut squash soup is that it is spiced with cilantro and green onions—ingredients that instantly transport me back home.

I always ask my mother to make this soup for me when she comes to Canada, and it's the one I crave most when feeling a bit homesick. It's truly food for the soul.

1. In a large pot, bring the vegetable stock to a boil over medium-high heat. Add the pumpkin and boil until fork-tender, about 18 minutes.

2. Meanwhile, in a large frying pan, heat the olive oil over medium heat. Add the Spanish onions, green onions, garlic, ½ cup (125 mL) of the cilantro, salt, and pepper. Cook, stirring frequently, until the onions are translucent and slightly browned, about 7 minutes. Remove from the heat.

3. Carefully ladle the cooked pumpkin with the vegetable stock into a high-speed blender. Add the onion mixture. (You will likely have to do this in a couple of batches.) Blend on high speed until smooth. Pour the soup back into the pot.

4. Stir the remaining 1 cup (250 mL) cilantro into the soup and simmer over medium heat until fragrant, about 10 minutes. Add the Parmesan and stir until melted.

5. Ladle the soup into bowls and top with more Parmesan, cilantro, and the pepitas. Store in a covered container in the fridge for up to 4 days or in the freezer for up to 1 month.

Green Goddess Soup

Serves 6

Vegetarian restaurants in Mexico City have been gaining popularity for a while now. A country that's well known for its meat dishes has made vegetarian food popular and more widely available. At Eno, one of my favourite restaurants in the Polanco neighbourhood, soup's on for lunch every day. When I lived in Mexico City, I would often stop there for lunch, especially to enjoy their creamy soups. Made with a variety of vegetables, this green goddess soup is packed with nutrients, and its fragrant spices give it the most wonderful flavour and aroma. It is a great way to get your kids to eat their vegetables, too!

2 tablespoons (30 mL) extra-virgin olive oil

1½ Spanish onions, chopped

5 cloves garlic, finely minced

1 teaspoon (5 mL) sea salt

1 teaspoon (5 mL) freshly ground pepper

1 teaspoon (5 mL) ground cumin

1 teaspoon (5 mL) ground coriander

1 teaspoon (5 mL) sweet paprika

½ teaspoon (2 mL) ground ginger

1 large bunch broccoli, cut into florets

2 medium zucchini, cut in ½-inch (1 cm) rounds

2 leeks (white and light green parts only), chopped, more for garnish

5 asparagus spears, trimmed

¾ cup (175 mL) canned cannellini beans, drained and rinsed

8 cups (2 L) vegetable stock

1 cup (250 mL) tightly packed fresh flat-leaf parsley leaves

½ cup (125 mL) tightly packed fresh basil leaves, more for garnish

1. In a large pot, heat the olive oil over medium heat. Add the onions, garlic, salt, pepper, cumin, coriander, paprika, and ginger. Cook, stirring often, until the onions are soft and translucent, about 7 minutes.

2. Add the broccoli, zucchini, leeks, asparagus, cannellini beans, and vegetable stock. Bring to a boil over high heat, then reduce the heat to medium. Add the parsley and basil and cook until the vegetables are fork-tender, about 12 minutes.

3. Carefully ladle the soup into a high-speed blender. (You will likely have to do this in a couple of batches.) Blend on high speed until smooth.

4. Pour the soup back into the pot and simmer over medium heat for 5 minutes.

5. Ladle the soup into bowls and garnish with basil and leeks. Store in a covered container in the fridge for up to 3 days or in the freezer for up to 1 month.

Curried Lentil Soup

Serves 6

As soon as the leaves start turning all shades of orange, soups become essential in our home. This curried lentil soup was inspired by the stewed pigeon peas ladled over rice that I enjoyed when growing up in Dominican Republic. Pigeon peas can be hard to find in North America, so here I've swapped them for lentils, adding a touch of curry for flavours. Fragrant cilantro from my beloved island infuses the soup with comforting aromas, and butternut squash provides creaminess without the need to add any cream. This soup is such a favourite at home, and I hope it becomes one in yours as well.

2 tablespoons (30 mL) extra-virgin olive oil

1½ white onions, finely chopped

4 cloves garlic, finely minced

3 green onions (white and light green parts only), finely chopped

1½ teaspoons (7 mL) sea salt

1½ teaspoons (7 mL) curry powder

1 teaspoon (5 mL) ground cumin

1 teaspoon (5 mL) freshly ground pepper

½ teaspoon (2 mL) ground coriander

1 cup (250 mL) peeled butternut squash cut in small cubes

1 cup (250 mL) red lentils

½ cup (125 mL) brown lentils

6 cups (1.5 L) vegetable stock

1 cup (250 mL) tightly packed fresh cilantro leaves, divided

1 cup (250 mL) crumbled feta cheese

1. In a large pot, heat the olive oil over medium heat. Add the white onions and cook, stirring often, until soft and translucent, about 7 minutes.

2. Add the garlic and cook, stirring constantly, until fragrant, about 30 seconds. Add the green onions, salt, curry, cumin, pepper, and coriander and cook, stirring constantly, for 1 minute.

3. Add the butternut squash and lentils and cook for 2 minutes, stirring occasionally. Increase the heat to medium-high. Add the vegetable stock and ½ cup (125 mL) of the cilantro, stir, and bring to a boil. Reduce the heat to medium, cover with a lid, and simmer until the lentils are tender, about 40 minutes.

4. Ladle 1 cup (250 mL) of the soup into a high-speed blender. Blend on high speed until smooth, then pour the puréed soup back into the pot. Reheat, stirring occasionally.

5. Ladle the soup into bowls and top with the remaining ½ cup (125 mL) cilantro and a sprinkle of feta. Store in a covered container in the fridge for up to 4 days or in the freezer for up to 1 month.

Black Bean and Chipotle Soup

Serves 6

Black beans are a staple in the Caribbean. Go to any Dominican, Cuban, or Puerto Rican home and odds are there's probably a big pot of black beans slowly cooking on the stove. On a trip to Havana, where gastronomy has been flourishing and new ingredients are suddenly appearing in classic dishes, I had a black bean soup that I knew I had to make when I got back home. It had the perfect trilogy of onions, garlic, and cilantro, but also a kick of spice. I've added chipotle peppers, which add a bit of spice with some smokiness, too. This black bean soup is wonderful topped with a dollop of sour cream.

3 tablespoons (45 mL) extra-virgin olive oil

1 tablespoon (15 mL) tomato paste

1 white onion, coarsely chopped

3 green onions (white and light green parts only), coarsely chopped

4 cloves garlic, finely minced

2 teaspoons (10 mL) sea salt

1½ teaspoons (7 mL) ground cumin

1 teaspoon (5 mL) ground coriander

1 teaspoon (5 mL) chipotle chili powder

2 cans (19 ounces/540 mL each) black beans, drained and rinsed

7½ cups (1.875 L) vegetable stock

1½ cups (375 mL) tightly packed fresh cilantro leaves, more for garnish

3 corn tortillas

½ cup (125 mL) full-fat sour cream

1. Preheat the oven to 375°F (190°C). Line a baking sheet with parchment paper.

2. In a large pot, heat the olive oil over medium heat. Add the tomato paste and cook, stirring constantly, for 1 minute.

3. Add the white onion and green onions and cook, stirring often, until the onions are soft and translucent, about 4 minutes. Stir in the garlic, salt, cumin, coriander, chili powder, and black beans and cook, stirring often, for 2 minutes.

4. Increase the heat to medium-high. Pour in the vegetable stock and stir in the cilantro. Cover with a lid and cook for 10 minutes.

5. Carefully ladle the soup into a high-speed blender. (You will likely have to do this in a couple of batches.) Blend until smooth.

6. Pour the soup back into the pot and simmer over medium-low heat for 15 minutes.

7. Meanwhile, cut the tortillas into thin strips and arrange on the baking sheet. Bake for 8 minutes, until golden brown and crisp, turning halfway through.

8. Ladle the soup into bowls and top with a dollop of sour cream, tortilla strips, and a sprinkle of cilantro leaves. Store the soup (without the toppings) in a covered container in the fridge for up to 3 days or in the freezer for up to 1 month.

Moroccan Stew with Spiced Chickpeas

Serves 6

1 cup (250 mL) freekeh

4 cups (1 L) water

3 tablespoons (45 mL)
  extra-virgin olive oil, divided

1½ yellow onions, finely diced

1 large carrot, peeled and
  finely diced

1 stalk celery, finely diced

4 cloves garlic, finely minced

1½ teaspoons (7 mL) sea salt

1 teaspoon (5 mL) freshly
  ground pepper

1 teaspoon (5 mL) coriander
  seeds

1 teaspoon (5 mL) ground
  cardamom

1 teaspoon (5 mL) nutmeg

1 teaspoon (5 mL) sweet
  paprika

1 teaspoon (5 mL) ground
  cloves

1 can (28 ounces/796 mL)
  crushed tomatoes

1 can (28 ounces/796 mL)
  chickpeas, drained and
  rinsed

1½ teaspoons (7 mL) ground
  cumin

For serving

¾ cup (175 mL) plain full-fat
  Greek yogurt

½ cup (125 mL) tightly packed
  chopped fresh flat-leaf
  parsley leaves

1 tablespoon (15 mL) lemon
  zest

Because of its proximity to Morocco, Barcelona's food gets a lot of influence from North African flavours. On many visits to Barcelona, I've found these flavours in all kinds of dishes, from soups to egg-based dishes to rice dishes. It's from that zesty and unforgettable palate that this Moroccan stew was born—an utterly delicious vegetarian dish that combines nutty freekeh and wholesome chickpeas in a fragrantly spiced tomato sauce. I've topped it with tangy Greek yogurt because its creaminess is simply glorious when mixed into this hearty stew.

1. Preheat the oven to 400°F (200°C). Line a baking sheet with parchment paper.

2. In a medium saucepan, combine the freekeh and water. Bring to a boil over high heat, then reduce the heat to medium-low and simmer for 25 minutes, or until the freekeh is tender and has absorbed the water.

3. In a large pot, heat 2 tablespoons (30 mL) of the olive oil over medium heat. Add the onions, carrot, and celery and cook, stirring often, until the onions are translucent and slightly brown, about 8 minutes.

4. Stir in the garlic, salt, pepper, coriander seeds, cardamom, nutmeg, paprika, and cloves. Cook, stirring constantly, for 1 minute.

5. Add the tomatoes, reduce the heat to low, and cook for 12 minutes.

6. Add the freekeh to the tomato mixture. Stir to combine and cover with a lid to keep warm.

7. Evenly spread the chickpeas on the prepared baking sheet. Drizzle with the remaining 1 tablespoon (15 mL) olive oil and sprinkle with the cumin and a little salt. Bake for 10 minutes, or until the chickpeas are crispy, stirring halfway through.

8. To serve, ladle the stew into bowls and top with a dollop of yogurt, roasted chickpeas, and a sprinkle each of parsley and lemon zest.

Mexican Tortilla Soup

Serves 4

Soups are a staple in our home as soon as autumn's chilly weather rolls in, especially this Mexican tortilla soup that my family loved when we lived in Mexico City. During the winter we would make this comforting and fiery soup after a trip to the nearby farmers' market. Roasted tomatoes and pasilla chilies are the two main ingredients in the broth, but in this version I've used chili powder and chipotle chili powder, since pasilla chilies are not easily found outside Mexico. Finally, it's the crispy tortilla strips, avocado, and cilantro that make this soup a favourite in my books, bringing back fond Mexico memories.

12 Roma tomatoes, cut in half lengthwise

1½ Spanish onions, coarsely chopped

3 tablespoons (45 mL) extra-virgin olive oil

1 teaspoon (5 mL) sea salt

4 cloves garlic, finely minced

7 cups (1.75 L) vegetable stock

½ teaspoon (2 mL) chili powder

½ teaspoon (2 mL) chipotle chili powder

2 green onions (white and green parts only), cut in half crosswise

1½ cups (375 mL) tightly packed fresh cilantro leaves, divided

4 corn tortillas

¼ cup (60 mL) Mexican crema or full-fat sour cream

2 avocados, pitted, peeled, and sliced

3 radishes, thinly sliced

1 lime, cut in half

1. Preheat the oven to 375°F (190°C). Line a baking sheet with foil.

2. Spread the tomatoes (cut side up) and onions on the prepared baking sheet. Drizzle with the olive oil and sprinkle with the salt. Roast for 27 minutes, stirring every 10 minutes. Scatter the garlic over the vegetables and roast for another 3 minutes. Set aside to cool, leaving the oven on.

3. Scrape the tomatoes and onions into a high-speed blender and add the vegetable stock. Blend on low speed for 30 seconds, then increase the speed to high and blend until smooth.

4. Pour the soup into a large pot. Stir in the chili powder, chipotle powder, green onions, and 1 cup (250 mL) of the cilantro. Bring to a boil, then reduce the heat and simmer for 10 minutes.

5. Meanwhile, line a baking sheet with parchment paper. Cut the tortillas into thin strips or triangles and arrange them on the baking sheet. Bake for 8 minutes, or until golden brown, turning halfway through.

6. Ladle the soup into bowls and top each serving with about 1 tablespoon (15 mL) of the Mexican crema, tortilla strips, avocado slices, radish slices, some of the remaining ½ cup (125 mL) cilantro, and a squeeze of lime juice. Store the soup (without the toppings) in a covered container in the fridge for up to 3 days or in the freezer for up to 1 month.

continued

Tip Mexican crema is a slightly sour condiment that falls somewhere between sour cream and crème fraîche. It has a hint of lime flavour and it's delicious over soups and tacos. If Mexican crema is not available at your local grocery store, you can use full-fat sour cream instead.

Pasilla chilies are one of the most popular chilies in Mexico and are used in salsas, sopa de tortilla and mole. They're fairly mild, with an earthy flavour. If you find them, replace the chili powder and chipotle chili powder with 1 pasilla chili. Before using, soak the chili in hot water for a few minutes to soften. Purée with the tomatoes.

Eggplant Escabeche

Serves 4

1 large Italian eggplant, peeled and cut into 1-inch (2.5 cm) cubes

1 tablespoon (15 mL) + ½ teaspoon (2 mL) sea salt, divided

1 medium Spanish onion, thinly sliced

1 sweet red pepper, thinly sliced lengthwise

½ cup (125 mL) + 1 tablespoon (15 mL) extra-virgin olive oil, divided

¼ teaspoon (1 mL) freshly ground pepper

2 cloves garlic, thinly sliced

3 tablespoons (45 mL) fresh lemon juice

Crusty bread or crackers, for serving

Buenos Aires has to be one of the most beautiful cities I've ever visited. Not only is the architecture stunning, modelled after Parisian architecture, but the food is absolutely luscious. If you are a vegetarian like me, be prepared to feast on savoury empanadas and velvety smooth fresh pasta.

In the early nineteenth century there was a vast migration from Italy to Argentina, which influenced the cuisine, including the way vegetables were preserved. One method is escabeche, pickling cooked or blanched vegetables or seafood in a mixture of olive oil and lemon or vinegar. This eggplant escabeche was inspired by the ones I've enjoyed during my many visits to Buenos Aires to visit relatives, and it's the one I make during hot summer evenings to have with some Manchego cheese and crusty bread. This eggplant melts in your mouth. This mouth-watering appetizer is easy to put together and can be made ahead. Believe me when I say it will be a recipe you'll be making over and over again.

1. Preheat the oven to 400°F (200°C). Line a baking sheet with parchment paper.

2. Place the eggplant in a colander over a large bowl or in the sink. Sprinkle with 1 tablespoon (15 mL) of the salt. Let sit for 10 minutes, or until beads of moisture start to form on the eggplant. Rinse under cold water to remove the excess salt, then drain. Press the eggplant cubes between kitchen towels to extract as much liquid as possible. Set aside.

3. Spread the Spanish onion and red pepper on the prepared baking sheet. Drizzle with 1 tablespoon (15 mL) of the olive oil and sprinkle with salt and pepper. Roast for 10 minutes, or until the pepper skins start to blister. Sprinkle the garlic over the vegetables and bake for another 2 minutes.

4. Meanwhile, half fill a medium pot with water and bring to a boil. Add the remaining ½ teaspoon (2 mL) salt and gently drop the eggplant into the water. Boil for 6 minutes, or just until the eggplant is soft. Drain and let cool for 5 minutes.

continued

5. Place the eggplant in a medium bowl. Add the roasted vegetable mixture. Pour in the remaining ½ cup (125 mL) olive oil and the lemon juice. Fold together to evenly coat the vegetables.

6. Enjoy at room temperature with crusty bread or crackers. Store in a covered container in the fridge for up to 2 weeks. Before serving, bring to room temperature.

Baked Feta with Spicy Tomato Sauce

Serves 6

The Plaka neighbourhood of Athens is incredibly picturesque. Look up and you'll be able to see the ancient Acropolis, a view that, no matter how many times I see it, still blows me away. Plaka's cobblestone streets are lined with olive trees. The sounds of clinking wine glasses and laughter spill from its many restaurants.

One of the dishes I order every time I visit is baked feta in tomato sauce spiced with oregano and fresh basil. I fell in love with this simple dish at the first bite, and at home I love baking it on summer evenings to serve with baked pita chips and a chilled glass of wine.

3 tablespoons (45 mL) extra-virgin olive oil, divided

½ white onion, finely chopped

3 cloves garlic, finely minced

2 tablespoons (30 mL) dried oregano, divided

1 teaspoon (5 mL) hot paprika

½ teaspoon (2 mL) sea salt

½ teaspoon (2 mL) freshly ground pepper

½ cup (125 mL) tightly packed fresh basil leaves

3 vine-ripened or Roma tomatoes, coarsely chopped

1 can (14 ounces/398 mL) crushed tomatoes

14 ounces (400 g) feta cheese, cut into 3 slices 1 inch (2.5 cm) thick

3 medium pita breads

⅓ cup (75 mL) tightly packed fresh flat-leaf parsley leaves

1. Preheat the oven to 350°F (180°C). Line a baking sheet with parchment paper.

2. In a large oven-safe frying pan, heat 2 tablespoons (30 mL) of the olive oil over medium heat. Add the onion and cook, stirring frequently, until soft and translucent, about 5 minutes.

3. Stir in the garlic and cook, stirring constantly, for 20 seconds. Sprinkle 1 tablespoon (15 mL) of the oregano, paprika, salt, pepper, and basil over the mixture and cook for 30 seconds, stirring constantly, until the herbs are fragrant.

4. Stir in the fresh tomatoes and cook for 1 minute, stirring halfway through. Add the crushed tomatoes, reduce the heat to low, and simmer for 5 minutes.

5. Arrange the feta slices over the tomato sauce. Sprinkle the remaining 1 tablespoon (15 mL) oregano over the feta. Transfer to the oven and bake for 12 minutes, or until the feta is slightly golden.

6. Cut the pita breads into large triangles. Arrange on the prepared baking sheet and drizzle with the remaining 1 tablespoon (15 mL) olive oil. Bake for 6 minutes, or until golden brown, turning halfway through.

7. Sprinkle parsley over the feta and serve hot with the pita chips on the side.

Traditional Mexican Guacamole

Serves 4 to 6

8 Hass avocados, cut in half, pitted, and peeled

6 cherry tomatoes, coarsely chopped

½ fresh or pickled jalapeño pepper, finely diced

½ clove garlic, finely minced

¾ cup (175 mL) loosely packed fresh cilantro leaves

⅓ cup (75 mL) finely diced red onion

2 tablespoons (30 mL) fresh lemon juice

1 tablespoon (15 mL) extra-virgin olive oil

Sea salt

Tortilla chips, for serving

You don't have to walk far in any Mexican city to find good guacamole. It is a perfect example of one of those dishes that only takes a handful of ingredients to be incredibly delicious. During our three-year stay in Mexico City, my family and I were fortunate to eat it often, piling mounds of it on everything from enchiladas and tostadas to huevos rancheros.

In Mexico, guacamole is traditionally made in a molcajete, the Mexican version of the mortar and pestle. Spiced with lots of cilantro, jalapeño peppers, and red onion, this traditional Mexican guacamole is tangy, spicy, and all-round full of delightful and zesty flavours. It's the perfect topping on my Shrimp Tacos with Chipotle Crema (page 206). Or simply enjoy it with tortilla chips, as here.

1. In a medium bowl (or molcajete, if you have one), slightly mash the avocados with a fork or potato masher, leaving visible chunks of avocado.

2. Using a rubber spatula, mix in the tomatoes, jalapeño, garlic, cilantro, red onion, lemon juice, olive oil, and salt to taste.

3. Transfer to a serving dish and enjoy with tortilla chips.

Zucchini and Quinoa Fritters with Tzatziki

Serves 8

Zucchini fritters are by far my favourite Greek dish. These light-as-air tasty morsels are the first thing I order to start a meal in Athens. Always served with garlicky tzatziki, they are the perfect starter. Grated zucchini is mixed with herbs, eggs, and spices, shaped into small patties, and lightly fried. Back home in Canada, I make them as a side dish, adding quinoa and feta to the batter to make these classic fritters heartier and add more nutritional value, too. You can enjoy the fritters on their own, or serve them topped with a poached egg for a lavish weekend brunch.

2 tablespoons (30 mL) extra-virgin olive oil, more for drizzling

1 yellow onion, finely chopped

3 cloves garlic, finely minced

½ cup (125 mL) tightly packed chopped fresh basil

½ cup (125 mL) tightly packed fresh flat-leaf parsley leaves

½ teaspoon (2 mL) sea salt

½ teaspoon (2 mL) freshly cracked pepper

2 small zucchini, grated on large holes of a box grater

1 cup (250 mL) cooked white quinoa, cooled

¾ cup (175 mL) whole wheat flour

¼ cup (60 mL) crumbled feta cheese

1 teaspoon (5 mL) baking powder

1 egg, lightly beaten

1½ cups (375 mL) panko crumbs

1 cup (250 mL) tzatziki

1. In a medium frying pan, heat the olive oil over medium-high heat. Add the onion and cook, stirring often, until translucent and brown, about 5 minutes.

2. Stir in the garlic, basil, parsley, salt, and pepper and cook for 1 minute, until the herbs and garlic are fragrant.

3. Scrape the herb mixture into a medium bowl. Add the zucchini, quinoa, flour, feta, baking powder, and egg. Mix until well combined. Let sit in the fridge for 30 minutes. This will ensure the patties hold their shape when baking.

4. Meanwhile, preheat the oven to 400°F (200°C). Line a baking sheet with parchment paper.

5. Spread the panko on a plate. Scoop ½ cup (125 mL) quinoa mixture per fritter and, using your hands, form into a small patty. Coat one side of a patty with the panko, gently turn, and coat the other side with the panko. Shake off any excess panko and place the patty on the prepared baking sheet. Repeat to make the remaining patties.

6. Drizzle a bit of olive oil over the patties and bake for 20 minutes, or until golden brown, turning them halfway through.

7. Serve the fritters hot with a generous dollop of tzatziki.

Roasted Asparagus with Egg and Toasted Almonds

Serves 4

My first time in Paris was magical. My partner, Warren, and I stayed in a light-filled apartment in the second arrondissement, just a few steps from Le Marais. We spent our days walking everywhere, having picnics, and visiting fromageries to learn about different kinds of cheese. We cherished the café culture in Paris, especially its simple yet satisfying lunches. One of my favourites was a plate of grilled asparagus topped simply with eggs. My version adds fragrant toasted almonds and a drizzle of balsamic vinegar. I love having this dish with grilled shrimp on the side if I am making it for dinner at home, but it's also satisfying on its own.

24 asparagus spears, trimmed

2 tablespoons (30 mL) extra-virgin olive oil, divided

1 tablespoon (15 mL) balsamic vinegar

2 eggs, hard-boiled

¼ cup (60 mL) slivered or sliced raw almonds, toasted

¼ teaspoon (1 mL) sea salt

¼ teaspoon (1 mL) freshly ground pepper

1. Preheat the oven to 350°F (180°C). Line a baking sheet with parchment paper.

2. Arrange the asparagus on the prepared baking sheet. Drizzle with 1 tablespoon (15 mL) of the olive oil. Roast until the asparagus is tender and slightly golden, about 10 minutes.

3. Arrange the asparagus on a platter and drizzle with the balsamic vinegar.

4. Grate the eggs on the large holes of a box grater. Sprinkle the egg over the asparagus and top with the remaining 1 tablespoon (15 mL) olive oil, toasted almonds, salt, and pepper. Serve hot.

Roasted Cauliflower Steaks over Garlicky Tomato Sauce with Toasted Almonds

Serves 4

1 large head cauliflower, sliced lengthwise through the core into 4 steaks ½ inch (1 cm) thick

2 tablespoons (30 mL) + 1½ teaspoons (7 mL) extra-virgin olive oil, divided

½ teaspoon (2 mL) ground cumin

¼ teaspoon (1 mL) coarse sea salt

¼ teaspoon (1 mL) pepper

½ yellow onion, finely chopped

2 cloves garlic, finely minced

½ teaspoon (2 mL) fine sea salt

½ teaspoon (2 mL) red chili flakes

¼ cup (60 mL) tightly packed fresh oregano leaves

2 Roma tomatoes, coarsely chopped

1 can (19 ounces/540 mL) crushed tomatoes

1 cup (250 mL) fresh breadcrumbs, toasted

1 cup (250 mL) slivered raw almonds, toasted

½ cup (125 mL) crumbled feta cheese

¾ cup (175 mL) finely chopped fresh basil

My take on cauliflower steaks was inspired by a visit to London, where after a full morning of walking, we sat down at one of my favourite restaurants in the city for lunch. They were zesty, herbaceous, and served with a bright green chimichurri sauce. Back home I found that a lightly spiced tomato sauce goes perfectly with it, especially when sprinkled with toasted almonds, creamy feta, and lightly toasted breadcrumbs. Feel free to enjoy this on its own or serve over quinoa, pasta, or brown rice. This dish takes little time to make, so it's ideal for busy nights.

1. Preheat the oven to 400°F (200 °C). Line a baking sheet with parchment paper.

2. Arrange the cauliflower steaks on the prepared baking sheet. Drizzle with 2 tablespoons (30 mL) of the olive oil and sprinkle with the cumin, coarse salt, and pepper. Roast until golden brown and charred bits can be seen on top, 14 to 16 minutes. Set aside.

3. In a large frying pan, heat the remaining 1½ teaspoons (7 mL) olive oil over medium heat. Add the onion and cook, stirring often, until translucent and slightly browned, about 7 minutes.

4. Add the garlic, fine salt, chili flakes, and oregano. Cook, stirring constantly, until fragrant, about 30 seconds. Stir in the fresh tomatoes and cook for 1 minute.

5. Stir in the canned tomatoes. Reduce the heat to low, cover with a lid, and simmer until the sauce has thickened, about 5 minutes.

6. Divide the tomato sauce among plates. Top with a cauliflower steak, breadcrumbs, almonds, feta, and basil.

Garlic Shrimp

Serves 4

Whenever I'm in Spain, I never pass up a chance to order *gambas al ajillo*, or garlic shrimp. On a trip to Madrid's San Miguel Market, a gourmet tapas market near Plaza Mayor, I had probably the best ones I've ever had. Served in little clay pots, the shrimp were tender and plump, the olive oil fragrantly laced with garlic and sherry. You can easily make this at home for a true taste of Spain. Just a handful of flavourful ingredients make these shrimp the ultimate tapa to make for friends on a Friday night. Garlicky, spicy, and delectable, and best enjoyed with crusty bread and a glass of chilled cava.

1½ pounds (675 g) large fresh shrimp, peeled and deveined

1 teaspoon (5 mL) sea salt

1¼ cups (300 mL) extra-virgin olive oil

5 cloves garlic, thinly sliced

1 small dried hot red chili pepper, seeds removed, crumbled

½ cup (125 mL) tightly packed finely minced fresh flat-leaf parsley leaves, more for serving

2 tablespoons (30 mL) dry sherry

Crusty bread, for serving

1. In a large bowl, toss the shrimp with the salt.

2. In a large, deep frying pan or medium Dutch oven, heat the olive oil over low heat. Add the garlic and cook, stirring occasionally, until fragrant and just starting to brown, about 8 minutes.

3. Add the crumbled chili pepper and cook, stirring constantly, until fragrant, about 20 seconds.

4. Increase the heat to medium-low. Add the shrimp and cook, stirring occasionally, until they turn pink, about 5 minutes.

5. Stir in the parsley, sherry, and a pinch of salt. Remove from the heat and let stand for 3 to 5 minutes. This allows the ingredients to release their flavours.

6. Divide among small bowls and top with parsley. Enjoy with crusty bread on the side.

Spanish Potato Tortilla

Serves 6

Go to any pintxo or tapas bar in Barcelona and you will find thick slices of *tortilla de patatas*, or Spanish omelette, on the menu. Thin slices of potatoes are mixed with slow-cooked onions and stirred into whisked eggs. The tortilla cooks in a frying pan, then is flipped onto a plate and sliced. At a tapas bar, you might find it served over a thick slice of baguette, or just on its own. At home in Canada, I often make it as a delicious and satisfying side dish. It pairs well with absolutely everything, from a simple green salad for lunch to salmon for dinner.

6 Yukon Gold potatoes, peeled and cut into ¼-inch (5 mm) slices

2½ teaspoons (12 mL) sea salt, divided, more to taste

1¾ cups (425 mL) +
2 tablespoons (30 mL)
extra-virgin olive oil, divided

1 medium Spanish onion, chopped

10 eggs, beaten

½ cup (125 mL) tightly packed fresh flat-leaf parsley leaves

For serving (optional)
Mayonnaise
Sweet paprika

1. Place the potatoes in a large colander set over a large bowl or in the sink. Sprinkle with 2 teaspoons (10 mL) of the salt and toss to coat. Let sit for 15 minutes. Pat dry with paper towels.

2. In a large nonstick frying pan, heat 1¾ cups (425 mL) of the olive oil over medium-high heat. Place the potatoes in the hot oil and cook, turning occasionally, until crisp and tender, 10 to 14 minutes.

3. Add the Spanish onion and cook, stirring often, until soft and translucent, about 5 minutes.

4. Using a slotted spoon, transfer the potatoes and onion to a large bowl. Add the eggs to the mixture and season with the remaining ½ teaspoon (2 mL) salt. Drain the oil and wipe the pan clean.

5. In the same pan, heat the remaining 2 tablespoons (30 mL) olive oil over medium-high heat. Pour the potato and onion mixture into the pan and using a spatula, spread it out evenly and smooth the top. Reduce the heat to medium-low and cook until the tortilla is golden on the bottom and almost set, about 12 minutes. It should still be slightly runny on top.

6. Invert the tortilla onto a large plate. Slide the tortilla back into the frying pan, browned side up. Cook until golden on the bottom, about 4 minutes.

7. Slide the tortilla onto a cutting board. Serve warm or at room temperature, topped with parsley and cut into wedges. Top wedges with a dab of mayonnaise and a sprinkle of paprika, if using.

Arugula, Pear, and Parmesan Salad

Serves 4

6 cups (1.5 L) loosely packed
  baby arugula

2 firm-ripe Bartlett pears,
  thinly sliced

1 cup (250 mL) raw walnuts,
  toasted

1½ cups (375 mL) shaved
  Parmesan cheese

3 tablespoons (45 mL)
  extra-virgin olive oil

3 tablespoons (45 mL)
  balsamic vinegar

¼ teaspoon (1 mL) freshly
  ground pepper

The streets of Florence are probably the most charming ones I've encountered in Italy. Leave the busy streets around the cathedral and you'll find yourself in quiet neighbourhood piazzas, where you'll discover incredibly delicious Tuscan cuisine. This salad was inspired by the flavours of a zesty Parmesan cheese that I had when I visited. It was served with peppery greens and a luscious balsamic glaze. This brilliant combination inspired me to create a salad that combined those savoury ingredients, plus pears for a hint of sweetness to balance it all out. This is one of my favourite salads, the perfect side with my Sesame and Maple Glazed Salmon (page 192).

1. Arrange the arugula on a platter or in a large bowl. Top with the pear slices, walnuts, and Parmesan. Drizzle with the olive oil and balsamic vinegar, and sprinkle with the pepper. Gently toss to combine.

Burrata and Grilled Nectarine Salad

Serves 4

3 tablespoons (45 mL)
extra-virgin olive oil, divided

4 nectarines, peeled and cut in
thick slices

¾ cup (175 mL) tightly packed
fresh mint leaves

3 tablespoons (45 mL)
balsamic vinegar

1 ball fresh burrata cheese
(about 8 ounces/225 g)

Sea salt

Freshly ground pepper

Toasted slices of baguette, for
serving (optional)

My first trip to Venice was very emotional. Ever since I was six, I'd dreamed of going to Italy. The sound of the language was music to my ears, and even at that young age, Italian architecture called my name. When I found myself in a gondola, and later that afternoon, standing in the middle of Piazza San Marco, I couldn't help but tear up. There is such a beauty in dreams coming true.

Once I discovered my passion for food, some of the first recipes I made were, of course, Italian. I particularly loved cheeses like Fontina, Parmigiano, and fresh mozzarella di bufala. That was, until I tasted burrata. Its tender shell of mozzarella is filled with stracciatella—mozzarella shreds—and cream, which ooze out when the cheese is cut. Pairing burrata with cherry tomatoes and basil is classic, but I invite you to pair it with grilled nectarines and mint. You'll thank me!

1. In a large grill pan, heat 1 tablespoon (15 mL) of the olive oil over medium heat. Arrange the nectarine slices in the pan without crowding them and cook, turning once, until grill marks appear on both sides. (You can also grill them on a barbecue, brushing the nectarine slices with olive oil before placing them on the hot grill.)

2. Transfer the nectarines to a medium bowl. Add the mint, balsamic vinegar, and the remaining 2 tablespoons (30 mL) olive oil. Using a rubber spatula, fold together to mix.

3. Place the burrata in the middle of a serving plate. Arrange the nectarine and mint mixture around the burrata. Sprinkle with a pinch each of salt and pepper. Enjoy on its own or serve with toasted slices of baguette on the side.

Watermelon, Strawberry, Mint, and Halloumi Salad

Serves 4

1 package (8.8 ounces/250 g)
 halloumi cheese, cut in
 ½-inch (1 cm) slices

12 slices watermelon, cut in
 triangles ¼ inch (5 mm) thick

½ cup (125 mL) fresh
 strawberries, cut in half

½ cup (125 mL) tightly packed
 fresh mint leaves

3 tablespoons (45 mL)
 extra-virgin olive oil

2 tablespoons (30 mL)
 balsamic vinegar

¼ teaspoon (1 mL) freshly
 ground pepper

The colourful streets of Aegina, an island near Athens, are lined with lush bougainvillea trees. Their deep magenta flowers drape over the white-painted buildings throughout the summer—a sight to remember. During the summer, locals pair fresh fruits with salty halloumi cheese, a combination I'm always drawn to. My version of this salad pairs sweet and juicy strawberries and refreshing watermelon with freshly grilled halloumi. The balsamic vinegar intensifies the flavours of the fruit, bringing out even more of its natural sweetness. This salad is the definition of summer on a plate. Perfect on its own or as a side dish for your next barbecue.

1. In a medium frying pan, fry the halloumi slices over medium heat until golden brown, about 1 minute per side.

2. Arrange the watermelon triangles on a platter. Scatter the strawberries over and between the watermelon, then scatter the halloumi and mint leaves on top.

3. Drizzle with the olive oil and balsamic vinegar. Sprinkle with pepper.

Grilled Provolone with Oregano and Tomatoes

Serves 4

2 slices provolone cheese
(1 inch/2.5 cm thick)

2 tablespoons (30 mL) dried
oregano

12 grape tomatoes, cut in half

¼ teaspoon (1 mL) sea salt

8 fresh basil leaves, for garnish

Crusty baguette, for serving
(optional)

When Argentinians have *asados*—a barbecue—it's served with a variety of salads and grilled vegetables. As someone who doesn't eat meat, my favourite part of the *asados* is provoleta with oregano and tomatoes. Thick slices of this local provolone-type cheese are melted on a grill or in an oven and topped generously with oregano, grape tomatoes, and basil. The cheese melts to perfection, forming a golden, bubbly crust on top. The oregano gives it a wonderful aroma, and it's absolutely delicious with slices of crusty bread and a glass of Malbec. I like to bake it in the oven, using small cast-iron pans that are ideal for sharing. It can also be baked in small baking dishes, big enough to fit the provolone slices.

1. Preheat the oven to 450°F (230°C).

2. Place a slice of cheese in each of two 3½-inch (9 cm) cast-iron frying pans. Sprinkle with the oregano. Divide the tomatoes evenly and arrange on top of the cheese. Sprinkle with salt.

3. Bake until the cheese is melted, about 5 minutes. Switch the oven to broil. Broil for 1 minute, or until the cheese has a golden-brown crust. Let cool on a rack for 3 minutes.

4. Scatter the basil leaves on top and serve hot with crusty baguette, if using.

Autumn Farro Salad

Serves 6

2 cups (500 mL) farro

6 cups (1.5 L) water

1 tablespoon (15 mL) +
½ teaspoon (2 mL) sea salt,
divided

1 medium acorn squash, cut
crosswise into 6 slices and
seeds removed

⅓ cup (75 mL) + 2 tablespoons
(30 mL) extra-virgin olive oil,
divided

¼ teaspoon (1 mL) pepper

2 crisp apples (Honeycrisp,
Gala, or McIntosh), cut in
thin strips

4 green onions (white and
light green parts only),
chopped

1 pomegranate, seeded

1 cup (250 mL) tightly packed
fresh basil leaves

½ cup (125 mL) tightly packed
fresh flat-leaf parsley leaves

1 cup (250 mL) coarsely
chopped raw pecans, toasted

½ cup (125 mL) coarsely
chopped raw walnuts,
toasted

¼ cup (60 mL) balsamic
vinegar

Four ingredients was all it took for me to fall in love with a salad in Florence. My friend Carlos, a Barcelona-born chef I met while in Lima, had given me a thoughtfully curated list of restaurants I had to try. His top pick was Trattoria Sergio Gozzi, right near Piazza San Lorenzo. The restaurant was busy at lunchtime with locals enjoying homemade pasta and bistecca alla Fiorentina, this city's most iconic dish.

My friend Tyler and I shared a plate of picci (similar to spaghetti but thicker) with a garlicky tomato sauce, followed by a farro salad with white basil, tomatoes, and olive oil. Maybe the salad had a sprinkle of sea salt—who knows? But right then and there, I understood the power of just a few ingredients, if they are the best quality and cooked properly. In this case, the farro was perfectly nutty, doused with fruity olive oil. The basil had just been picked, and the tomatoes were sweet, plump, and all-round delicious. I didn't need to look any further for a reason to love Florence. This autumn salad has a few more ingredients but holds the essence of fresh and local ingredients, laced with a bouquet of fragrant herbs and olive oil.

1. Preheat the oven to 400°F (200°C). Line a baking sheet with parchment paper.

2. Rinse and drain the farro. In a large pot, bring the farro, water, and 1 tablespoon (15 mL) of the salt to a boil. Reduce the heat to medium-low and simmer until the farro is just tender, about 35 minutes. Drain any excess water and transfer the farro to a large bowl.

3. Meanwhile, place the squash on the prepared baking sheet. Drizzle with 2 tablespoons (30 mL) of the olive oil and sprinkle with the remaining ½ teaspoon (2 mL) salt and the pepper. Roast until fork-tender and golden brown, about 15 minutes, turning halfway through. Add to the farro.

4. Add the apples, green onions, pomegranate seeds, basil, parsley, pecans, walnuts, the remaining ⅓ cup (75 mL) olive oil, and the balsamic vinegar. Toss well to combine.

5. Enjoy at room temperature or cold. Store in a covered container in the fridge for up to 3 days.

Toronto

Travelling the world has shown me the beauty of different cultures and magical landscapes. It has gifted me with the joy of discovering countless cuisines and has opened my taste buds to an array of flavours. But nothing feels as good as home. Toronto's diversity gives the city a vibrancy like no other. The city's many cultures and inventive cuisines combine to create an unmatchable food scene.

Toronto is a city of neighbourhoods. One of my favourites is the bohemian Kensington Market, a lively community with deliciously diverse food, vintage stores, fruit and vegetable markets, and grocers. It is where I go when I want to buy Latin American ingredients that I can't find at my local grocery store, be it cotija or Oaxaca cheese from Mexico, coffee from Ecuador, or dulce de leche from seaside Mar del Plata in Argentina. Kensington Market is the purest example of how multicultural Toronto is. If you find yourself in the market, you can start by enjoying Swedish pastries and coffee at Fika, or if you crave something savoury, don't miss Golden Patty for their curry shrimp and Jamaican patties.

From Kensington Market you can stroll to Queen Street West, where the food options are endless. Korean, Mexican, Venezuelan, Argentinian, and Italian are just some of the many cuisines you'll come across.

Close to the downtown core, St. Lawrence Market is one of my go-to spots for buying ingredients. The market is home to two floors of merchants that sell a variety of fruits, vegetables, cheeses, meats, and seafood. There are also a few bakeries, including Carousel, where I get custardy *pastéis de nata* just like the ones I buy in Lisbon.

For dinner, all roads lead to Bar Raval. This Gaudí-inspired restaurant is my favourite for tapas. I enjoy going with my family on weekends and ordering tangy Manchego cheese, grilled shishito peppers sprinkled with salt, and *pan con tomate*, a Catalan specialty of toasted sourdough bread rubbed with garlic and fresh tomatoes.

Travel has enriched my soul, but there's nothing like coming home to a city that embraces the world, inspiring me daily.

Dinner

There's something so comforting about sitting around a table sharing a meal with friends and family. I live for moments where plates piled with delicious food are passed around and thoroughly savoured.

Before I travel, I usually do a bit of research into the local cuisine and learn which restaurants stand out. Sometimes it is the hole-in-the-wall spots where you find creativity in all its glory, where ingredients that are new to me make for a transformative experience. These flavours show you the true soul of a country and tell you the story of a city. Inspired by these memorable dishes, I feel excited every single time I come back home from my trips with countless ingredients to cook for our family dinners: Parmigiano-Reggiano and truffle oil from Venice, halloumi and feta cheese from Athens, sardines and piri-piri sauce from Lisbon, olive oil and Manchego cheese from Spain, and the sweetest mango and passion fruit from Lima. Treasures that infuse my cooking with the magic of travel.

Summer Caprese Salad with Garlic Ciabatta Croutons

Serves 4

1 day-old medium loaf ciabatta bread

1 large clove garlic, cut in half

5 tablespoons (75 mL) extra-virgin olive oil, divided

4 vine-ripened tomatoes, cut in half

4 cups (1 L) cherry tomatoes, cut in half

1 cup (250 mL) tightly packed fresh basil leaves

2 balls (8 ounces/225 g each) buffalo mozzarella cheese, sliced ¼ inch (5 mm) thick

Sea salt

One of my most treasured memories from my trip to Florence was having the most delicious bruschetta in a neighbourhood piazza one balmy evening. What made it so delicious? The tomatoes. Tomatoes in Italy are out of this world: deliciously sweet and perfectly ripe. This is the country that gave rise to the Slow Food movement, so the produce you eat at any restaurant would almost certainly come from a farm nearby. Obsessed with the taste of the tomatoes I had in Florence, I'm always on the lookout for the freshest ones I can find to make caprese salad in the summer. After all, summertime is made for easy meals that you can put together in no time with just a few ingredients.

My caprese salad has the classic main ingredients—velvety buffalo mozzarella, fragrant basil, and of course the best tomatoes you can find. What makes this caprese a little bit different is the addition of garlic ciabatta croutons. They give this iconic salad a heartier feel, making it perfect for dinner. Drizzle this salad with the best extra-virgin olive oil you can afford and be transported to Italy in no time.

1. Preheat the oven to 400°F (200°C). Line a baking sheet with parchment paper.

2. Cut the bread into thick slices. Rub each slice with the garlic, then cut the slices into 1-inch (2.5 cm) cubes. Discard the garlic clove. Spread the bread on the prepared baking sheet. Drizzle 2 tablespoons (30 mL) of the olive oil over the bread and toss until evenly coated. Bake until golden brown, about 5 minutes, turning halfway through.

3. Place the vine-ripened and cherry tomatoes on a platter. Scatter with the basil and mix together. Then scatter the mozzarella and croutons on top. Drizzle the remaining 3 tablespoons (45 mL) olive oil over the salad. Sprinkle with salt to taste and serve immediately.

Roasted Acorn Squash with Farro and Pistachios

Serves 4

The farm-to-table movement wouldn't be where it is today had it not been for Alice Waters, founder of Chez Panisse, the first restaurant in North America to cook its meals with the simple principle that everything tastes better when grown locally. Zuni Café followed suit, and both restaurants have made iconic dishes that are admired around the world for the simplicity of bringing the freshest produce to the table, making it the star ingredient.

This roasted acorn squash stuffed with farro and pistachios is inspired by the vegetarian meals I had while visiting San Francisco.

1 cup (250 mL) farro

3 cups (750 mL) water

2 teaspoons (10 mL) sea salt, divided

2 medium acorn squash, cut in half crosswise and seeds removed

3 tablespoons (45 mL) extra-virgin olive oil, divided

1 tablespoon (15 mL) pure maple syrup

½ cup (125 mL) finely diced red onion

3 cloves garlic, finely minced

Leaves of 2 thyme sprigs

1 sweet red pepper, finely diced

2 green onions (white and light green parts only), thinly sliced

2 cups (500 mL) thinly sliced cremini mushrooms

¼ teaspoon (1 mL) freshly cracked pepper

Zest and juice of 1 lemon

1 cup (250 mL) raw pistachios, toasted

1. Preheat the oven to 375°F (190°C). Line a baking sheet with parchment paper.

2. Rinse and drain the farro. In a large pot, bring the farro, water, and 1½ teaspoons (7 mL) of the salt to a boil. Reduce the heat to medium-low and simmer until the farro is just tender, about 35 minutes. Drain off any excess water and transfer the farro to a large bowl.

3. Using a sharp knife, trim the ends of the squash halves so they can stand upright. Place cut side up on the prepared baking sheet. Brush the top and insides of the squash with 2 tablespoons (30 mL) of the olive oil and the maple syrup. Sprinkle with ¼ teaspoon (1 mL) of the salt. Roast until the squash is tender and golden brown, 18 to 20 minutes. Let cool for 5 minutes.

4. Meanwhile, in a medium frying pan, heat the remaining 1 tablespoon (15 mL) olive oil over medium heat. Add the red onion and cook, stirring often, until soft and translucent, about 5 minutes.

5. Stir in the garlic and cook for 30 seconds. Stir in the thyme, red pepper, green onions, mushrooms, the remaining ¼ teaspoon (1 mL) salt, and pepper. Cook for 2 minutes, until the vegetables are tender but not entirely soft.

6. Add the vegetables, lemon zest and juice, and pistachios to the farro and stir to combine. Divide the farro and vegetable mixture equally among the squash halves and serve.

Cashew and Tofu Buddha Bowls

Serves 4

1½ cups (375 mL) white quinoa, rinsed

3 cups (750 mL) water

1¼ teaspoons (6 mL) sea salt, divided

¼ cup (60 mL) sesame oil

¼ cup (60 mL) tamari

¼ teaspoon (1 mL) freshly cracked pepper

1 block (10 ounces/300 g) extra-firm tofu

¼ cup (60 mL) cornstarch

⅓ cup (75 mL) + 1 tablespoon (15 mL) olive oil, divided

Juice of 1½ lemons

1 tablespoon (15 mL) Thai red curry paste

½ teaspoon (2 mL) pure maple syrup

1 clove garlic, finely minced

1 medium English cucumber, sliced

2 cups (500 mL) cherry tomatoes, cut in half

2 avocados, pitted, peeled, and thinly sliced

1 medium red onion, thinly sliced

4 radishes, thinly sliced

½ sweet red pepper, sliced into thin lengths

2 green onions (white and light green parts only), thinly sliced

1 cup (250 mL) whole raw cashews, toasted

Montreal's food scene is more vibrant every time I visit. Vegetarian and vegan restaurants are popping up everywhere. On one visit I had the most delicious Buddha bowl packed with fresh vegetables, brown rice, and almonds.

At home, I make my version by marinating the tofu in a sesame and tamari marinade that infuses it with tons of flavour. I also add creamy avocado and, for crunch, toasted cashews and radishes. To top it all off, a zesty red curry vinaigrette adds a tangy kick to one of my favourite go-to dinners.

1. Preheat the oven to 375°F (190°C). Line a baking sheet with parchment paper.

2. In a medium saucepan, combine the quinoa, water, and 1 teaspoon (5 mL) of the salt. Bring to a boil over medium-high heat. Reduce the heat to low, cover with a lid, and simmer for 12 to 14 minutes, until the quinoa is tender and has absorbed the water. Remove from the heat and fluff with a fork. Let sit, covered, until ready to use.

3. Meanwhile, in a medium bowl, whisk together the sesame oil, tamari, the remaining ¼ teaspoon (1 mL) salt, and pepper. Drain the tofu and pat dry with a kitchen towel. Cut into 2-inch (5 cm) cubes. Add the tofu to the marinade and toss to coat. Let marinate for 5 minutes.

4. Drain the marinade from the tofu. Sprinkle the cornstarch over the tofu and toss to coat. Drizzle 1 tablespoon (15 mL) of the olive oil over the tofu.

5. Arrange the tofu on the prepared baking sheet. Roast until golden brown, about 12 minutes, turning the cubes halfway through.

6. Meanwhile, in a medium bowl, combine the remaining ⅓ cup (75 mL) olive oil, lemon juice, curry paste, maple syrup, and garlic. Whisk until well blended.

7. To serve, scoop the quinoa into bowls. Top with the roasted tofu, cucumber, tomatoes, avocado, red onion, radishes, sweet peppers, green onions, and cashews. Drizzle with the dressing and serve immediately.

Quinoa Salad with Roasted Vegetables and Feta

Serves 4

1½ cups (375 mL) white
quinoa, rinsed

3 cups (750 mL) water

1 teaspoon (5 mL) sea salt,
divided

1 sweet red pepper, thinly
sliced

1 medium red onion,
thickly sliced

1 small eggplant, peeled and
cut into ½-inch (1 cm) cubes

1 cup (250 mL) cherry
tomatoes, cut in half

2 cloves garlic, coarsely
chopped

¼ cup (60 mL) + 2 tablespoons
(30 mL) extra-virgin olive oil,
divided

2 tablespoons (30 mL)
balsamic vinegar

½ teaspoon (2 mL) freshly
cracked pepper

½ teaspoon (2 mL) sweet
paprika

Juice of 1 lemon

¾ cup (175 mL) crumbled feta
cheese

2 green onions (white and light
green parts only), chopped

1 tablespoon (15 mL) sesame
seeds

¼ cup (60 mL) tightly packed
fresh basil leaves

Running has always been a very important part of my life.
I love creating nutritious meals like this quinoa salad to have
on hand when I run in the evenings. It is hearty and has tons
of texture and layers of flavour thanks to the saltiness and
creaminess of the feta cheese balanced by the sweetness of the
roasted peppers. When I lived in Mexico City, it was my go-to
with a piece of roasted fish, and now at home in Canada it's
what I make to have with my Sesame and Maple Glazed
Salmon (page 191). But it's also wonderful on its own.

1. Preheat the oven to 375°F (190°C). Line a baking sheet with
   parchment paper.

2. In a medium saucepan, combine the quinoa, water, and
   ½ teaspoon (2 mL) of the salt. Bring to a boil over medium-
   high heat. Reduce the heat to low, cover with a lid, and
   simmer for 12 to 14 minutes, until the quinoa is tender
   and has absorbed all the water. Remove from the heat and
   fluff with a fork. Let sit, covered, until ready to use.

3. Meanwhile, place the red pepper, red onion, eggplant,
   tomatoes, and garlic on the prepared baking sheet.
   Drizzle with ¼ cup (60 mL) of the olive oil and the
   balsamic vinegar. Sprinkle with the remaining ½ teaspoon
   (2 mL) salt, pepper, and paprika. Toss to coat. Spread evenly
   on the baking sheet and roast until the vegetables
   are fork-tender and the peppers are slightly charred,
   18 to 20 minutes, stirring halfway through.

4. Transfer the quinoa to a large bowl and mix in the roasted
   vegetables. Pour the lemon juice and the remaining
   2 tablespoons (30 mL) olive oil over the mixture. Mix with
   a spoon until the vegetables, quinoa, and dressing are well
   incorporated.

5. To serve, sprinkle with feta, green onions, sesame seeds,
   and basil. Enjoy hot or cold. Store in an airtight container
   in the fridge for up to 3 days.

Israeli Couscous with Pistachios, Kalamata Olives, and Goat Cheese

Serves 4

3 cups (750 mL) water

1 tablespoon (15 mL) +
½ teaspoon (2 mL) sea salt,
divided

1½ cups (375 mL) Israeli
couscous

½ large red onion, minced

1 can (19 ounces/540 mL)
chickpeas, drained and
rinsed

1½ cups (375 mL) tightly
packed finely chopped fresh
flat-leaf parsley leaves

¾ cup (175 mL) loosely packed
chopped fresh mint leaves

¾ cup (175 mL) large Kalamata
olives, pitted and sliced

1 teaspoon (5 mL) lemon zest

Juice of 1 lemon

¼ cup (60 mL) extra-virgin
olive oil

½ cup + 2 tablespoons (155 mL)
plain full-fat Greek yogurt

1 cup (250 mL) crumbled firm
goat cheese

1 cup (250 mL) raw pistachios,
toasted

1 teaspoon (5 mL) freshly
cracked pepper

My partner, Warren, and I spent two weeks one summer visiting friends in Melbourne, Australia, a city that instantly became one of my favourites for its unparalleled food scene. It's fair to say we ate our way through Melbourne. From its brunches laden with avocado and poached eggs to its Asian-influenced seafood dinners, Melbourne is not to be missed. One night, our host and friend Mark made us a spectacular salad chock full of pistachios, olives, and chickpeas. A creamy, herbaceous yogurt dressing tied these hearty ingredients together.

The moment we got back to Canada I set about making my own version. The yogurt dressing adds a luscious creaminess, and when paired with the mint and lemon, instantly makes this a stellar salad to serve at your next summer barbecue, potluck, or dinner with friends. You can have it on its own as a hearty vegetarian main dish, or as a side dish served with Piri-Piri Roasted Fish (page 209) or Sesame and Maple Glazed Salmon (page 192).

1. In a large saucepan, bring the water and 1 tablespoon (15 mL) of the salt to a boil. Pour the couscous into the boiling water and cook until just tender, about 15 minutes. Drain and let cool for 10 minutes.

2. In a medium bowl, combine the red onion, chickpeas, parsley, mint, olives, lemon zest, lemon juice, and olive oil. Mix well.

3. Add the couscous to the vegetables and stir with a spoon. Scoop the yogurt onto the couscous and fold in until all the ingredients are evenly coated with the yogurt.

4. Add the goat cheese, pistachios, the remaining ½ teaspoon (2 mL) salt, and pepper. Mix well. Enjoy at room temperature or cold. Store in an airtight container in the fridge for up to 2 days.

Mushroom Ragú over Creamy Polenta with Mascarpone

Serves 6

Creamy Polenta with Mascarpone

2 cups (500 mL) 2% milk

2 cups (500 mL) water

1 teaspoon (5 mL) sea salt

1 cup (250 mL) yellow cornmeal

⅓ cup (75 mL) mascarpone cheese

¼ cup (60 mL) whipping (35%) cream

¼ teaspoon (1 mL) freshly cracked pepper

Mushroom Ragú

2 tablespoons (30 mL) extra-virgin olive oil

1 tablespoon (15 mL) truffle oil

1 small Spanish onion, finely chopped

½ teaspoon (2 mL) sea salt

½ teaspoon (2 mL) freshly ground pepper

4 cloves garlic, finely minced

1½ pounds (675 g) mixed fresh mushrooms (such as enoki, oyster, button, shiitake, cremini), stems removed and coarsely chopped

¾ cup (175 mL) tightly packed chopped fresh flat-leaf parsley leaves, more for garnish

¾ cup (175 mL) finely grated Parmesan cheese

The first time I tried polenta, I was visiting family in Argentina. There was a beef ragú in the making to be lusciously spooned on top of the creamiest polenta I have ever eaten, served on a big wooden board from which everyone scooped it into bowls. I topped mine with a splash of cream and a delicious spoonful of freshly grated Parmesan cheese. The cheese melted as soon as it touched the hot polenta, blending in with this creamy goodness. This was the kind of meal that is made to share with family and friends.

Years later, while we lived in Mexico City, we took a weekend trip to the impossibly beautiful San Miguel de Allende, and polenta surprised me again. This time it was served with heaping spoonfuls of tomato sauce made from scratch and buffalo mozzarella. Sprinkled with fresh basil leaves, it was pure umami for the soul. After returning to Canada, I knew polenta would be the dish to make during cold winter nights, especially if topped with an earthy mix of mushrooms sautéed in olive oil, garlic, and parsley and topped with a shower of Parmesan cheese.

1. To make the creamy polenta with mascarpone: In a large pot, combine the milk, water, and salt and bring to a boil over medium-high heat.

2. Gradually whisk in the cornmeal. Reduce the heat to low and simmer for 16 minutes, until smooth and thick, stirring constantly to prevent lumps.

3. Stir in the mascarpone, cream, and pepper. Continue stirring for 2 minutes. Remove from the heat and set aside, keeping warm.

4. To make the mushroom ragú: In a large frying pan, heat the olive oil and truffle oil over medium heat. Add the onion, salt, and pepper and cook, stirring often, until soft and translucent, about 5 minutes.

continued

5. Add the garlic and cook for 30 seconds, stirring constantly. Add the mixed mushrooms and stir until the mushrooms are coated in oil and onions. Cover with a lid and cook for 4 minutes, stirring halfway through.

6. Stir in the parsley and cook, uncovered and stirring often, until the mushrooms have reduced in size and browned, about 3 minutes.

7. Spread the warm polenta on a wooden cutting board or spoon into bowls. Top with the mushroom ragú, parsley, and Parmesan.

Buenos Aires Crêpes

Crêpes

1 cup (250 mL) all-purpose
    flour

¼ teaspoon (1 mL) granulated
    sugar

¼ teaspoon (1 mL) sea salt

1½ cups (375 mL) 2% milk

4 eggs

3 tablespoons (45 mL) melted
    unsalted butter, more for
    cooking

Tomato Sauce

2 tablespoons (30 mL)
    extra-virgin olive oil

3 cloves garlic, finely minced

1 can (28 ounces/796 mL)
    crushed tomatoes

½ cup (125 mL) tightly packed
    fresh basil leaves, more
    for garnish

½ teaspoon (2 mL) dried
    oregano

½ teaspoon (2 mL) granulated
    sugar

½ teaspoon (2 mL) sea salt

½ teaspoon (2 mL) freshly
    ground pepper

My youngest daughter, Gaby, has family in Argentina, so we've been travelling to that beautiful country since she was just a few months old. Gatherings at night with family and friends often end with piping hot empanadas and gelato for dessert, but for lunch we used to order food from a woman who delivered homemade meals. She would bring butternut squash soup with grated Parmesan on top, or pan-fried sole over garlicky spinach with golden noisette potatoes. But what I always looked forward to were her paper-thin and tender crêpes filled with homemade ricotta and spinach and covered in the most delicious fresh tomato sauce.

In my version, these thin and delicate crêpes get a creamy ricotta, mascarpone, and spinach filling and are then bathed in a garlicky tomato sauce and topped with fresh mozzarella. It's such a comforting and delicious meal, perfect to enjoy with loved ones. You can make the crêpes a few days before to save a bit of time.

1. To make the crêpe batter: In a blender, combine the flour, sugar, salt, milk, eggs, and butter. Blend for about 30 seconds, until smooth and bubbles form on top. Let the batter sit for at least 15 minutes at room temperature. (You can make the batter up to 1 day ahead. Store in an airtight container in the fridge and whisk before using.)

2. Heat a medium nonstick frying pan over medium heat. Lightly coat the pan with butter. When it is melted, pour in ⅓ cup (75 mL) of the batter and swirl the pan to evenly cover the bottom. Cook until the bottom of the crêpe is golden brown, about 30 seconds. Loosen the edge of the crêpe with a rubber spatula, then with your fingers carefully flip the crêpe. Continue to cook for 1 minute. Carefully slide the crêpe onto a plate. Repeat with the remaining batter, coating the pan with butter before cooking each crêpe. Stack the crêpes, separating each crêpe with a piece of parchment paper so they don't stick together.

continued

Filling

2 packages (10 ounces/
   300 g each) frozen whole leaf
   spinach, thawed, drained,
   and squeezed to remove
   excess liquid

2 cups (500 mL) ricotta cheese

½ cup (125 mL) freshly grated
   Parmesan cheese

¼ cup (60 mL) mascarpone
   cheese

2 cloves garlic, finely minced

½ cup (125 mL) tightly packed
   chopped fresh flat-leaf
   parsley leaves

¼ teaspoon (1 mL) sea salt

¼ teaspoon (1 mL) freshly
   ground pepper

1 ball (8 ounces/225 g) fresh
   mozzarella cheese, sliced
   ¼ inch (5 mm) thick

3. To make the tomato sauce: In a medium saucepan, heat the olive oil over medium heat. Add the garlic and cook, stirring constantly, for 30 seconds. Add the crushed tomatoes, basil, oregano, sugar, salt, and pepper. Reduce the heat to low and simmer for 10 minutes.

4. Preheat the oven to 375°F (190°C).

5. To make the filling: In a medium bowl, combine the spinach, ricotta, Parmesan, mascarpone, garlic, parsley, salt, and pepper. Mix together with a rubber spatula.

6. To assemble the crêpes: Evenly spread ½ cup (125 mL) of the tomato sauce in a large baking dish.

7. Lay a crêpe on a work surface. Spoon ⅓ cup (75 mL) of the filling down the centre of the crêpe. From the longest side of the crêpe, roll each crêpe like a tube or jellyroll. Repeat to fill and roll the remaining crêpes.

8. Once all the crêpes have been placed in the baking dish, cover with the remaining tomato sauce. Top with slices of mozzarella. Cover with foil and bake for 35 minutes. Carefully remove the foil (the sauce will be bubbly) and bake for another 5 minutes, or until the cheese browns slightly and the sauce thickens a bit more.

9. Let sit for 10 minutes before serving. Just before serving, garnish with basil leaves.

Truffle Pasta with Mixed Mushrooms

Serves 8

1 pound (450 g) mafalde or fettuccine

2 tablespoons (30 mL) extra-virgin olive oil

2 tablespoons (30 mL) truffle oil

5 cloves garlic, thinly sliced

1 teaspoon (5 mL) freshly ground pepper

½ teaspoon (2 mL) sea salt

¾ pound (340 g) shiitake mushrooms, stems removed and coarsely chopped

½ pound (250 g) enoki mushrooms, stems removed and coarsely chopped

½ pound (250 g) portobello mushrooms, stems removed and thinly sliced

⅓ pound (170 g) cremini mushrooms, stems removed and thinly sliced

1 cup (250 mL) tightly packed fresh flat-leaf parsley leaves

2 cups (500 mL) whipping (35%) cream

1 cup (250 mL) freshly grated Parmesan cheese, more for serving

Because of Venice's location near the mountains and its colder weather during the winter months, some Venetian pasta sauces are hearty, rich, and often made with cream and butter. Serving fresh pasta with velvety smooth cream, garlic, and a sprinkle of Parmesan sounds too simple to be delicious, but it's the simplicity of recipes like this one that can make a bowl of pasta such a pleasure to eat. One day in Venice, I stopped for lunch near the Grand Canal and had a wild mushroom mafalde (a ribbon-shaped pasta, similar to fettuccine but with ruffles along both edges) with cream. The pasta was homemade, and the flavour of the porcini mushrooms infused the cream. After lunch, I went straight to a grocery store to buy the ingredients to recreate it at home.

When I can't find porcini mushrooms at the grocery store, I use a mix of portobello, shiitake, enoki, and cremini mushrooms along with a few tablespoons of truffle oil to bring me back to that afternoon in Venice.

1. Boil the pasta in a large pot of salted water until just tender, about 12 minutes. Reserve ¾ cup (175 mL) of the pasta water, then drain the pasta.

2. Meanwhile, in a large sauté pan with a lid, heat the olive oil and truffle oil over medium heat. Add the garlic and cook, stirring, until fragrant and slightly brown, about 1 minute. Add the pepper, salt, and all the mushrooms and stir to coat with the oils and garlic. Cover with the lid and cook until the mushrooms start to reduce in size, about 5 minutes.

3. Stir in the parsley and cream. Cook, uncovered, until the cream has thickened slightly, about 4 minutes. Stir in the Parmesan and cook for 1 minute more.

4. Using tongs, transfer the pasta to the pan. Add the reserved pasta water and toss to coat with the mushroom sauce.

5. To serve, divide among pasta bowls and top with a sprinkle of Parmesan.

Barcelona's Paella

Serves 8

¼ cup (60 mL) extra-virgin olive oil

1 large Spanish onion, finely chopped

5 cloves garlic, minced

1 tablespoon (15 mL) saffron threads

1½ teaspoons (7 mL) sweet paprika

1½ teaspoons (7 mL) sea salt

½ teaspoon (2 mL) freshly ground pepper

1 cup (250 mL) tightly packed fresh flat-leaf parsley leaves, divided

2½ cups (625 mL) bomba rice or other short-grain rice

5 cups (1.25 L) water

1 pound (450 g) large fresh shell-on shrimp, deveined

10 ounces (280 g) fresh baby scallops, side muscle removed

10 ounces (280 g) fresh mussels, scrubbed and beards removed

½ cup (125 mL) thawed frozen peas

1 sweet red pepper, thinly sliced

Growing up in Dominican Republic gave me my first insight into Spanish cuisine. The first island colonized by Christopher Columbus, in 1492, was heavily influenced by Spanish cuisine. When it comes to Dominican food, just about every dish, in true Spanish way, starts with onions and garlic. These two ingredients are the base for one of my favourite Spanish meals. As a child, I remember special celebrations called for paella, an aromatic dish made with bomba rice (a short-grain variety used for paella in Spain), meat or seafood, and tons of orange-hued saffron. When I started travelling to Barcelona and having my fair share of paella on every trip, I realized how the food we love is tied to our childhood.

This seafood paella couldn't be easier to make. An incredibly tasty one-pan meal, it's great for a Sunday lunch with family and friends. The rice cooks slowly with saffron-scented seafood, peas, and red peppers, absorbing all the flavours. Don't let the recipe intimidate you. It requires a bit of prep, but once the paella gets going the process is seamless and the rewards are huge.

1. In a paella pan or very large, deep frying pan, heat the olive oil over medium heat. Add the onion, garlic, saffron, paprika, salt, pepper, and ½ cup (125 mL) of the parsley. Cook, stirring often, until the onion is soft and translucent and the mixture is fragrant, about 7 minutes.

2. Add the rice and cook, stirring constantly, until well coated, about 2 minutes.

3. Pour in the water, reduce the heat to low, and cook for 8 minutes. The water will look slightly orange as the saffron starts releasing its colour.

4. Add the shrimp, scallops, mussels, and peas. Scatter the red pepper on top and cook, uncovered, until the mussels have opened, the shrimp are pink, and the rice is tender, about 35 minutes. Discard any mussels that did not open. Sprinkle the remaining ½ cup (125 mL) parsley on top. Serve hot.

Lemongrass Mussels

Serves 4

I grew up with the aroma of lemongrass lingering in the air of my father's medical practice. Deeply committed to health, he would have the staff at the clinic make lemongrass tea to serve to anyone visiting. To this day, the smell of lemongrass reminds me of summers when I helped out at his office. Later in life, I would come across lemongrass in my travels in local markets, but also in restaurants, where it was added to soups, stews, and fish curries.

This fragrant recipe combines lemongrass, garlic, chili flakes, parsley, and Sauvignon Blanc in a marvellous broth that pairs perfectly with the taste of the mussels without overpowering them. As a bonus, this mussel recipe is simple to put together and will be ready in just minutes. Enjoy with warm crusty bread to sop up the broth.

¼ cup (60 mL) extra-virgin olive oil

1 large Spanish onion, finely chopped

5 cloves garlic, thinly sliced

1 tablespoon (15 mL) grated lemongrass (white part only) or 1 tablespoon (15 mL) lemongrass paste

1 teaspoon (5 mL) sea salt

½ teaspoon (2 mL) red chili flakes

1 cup (250 mL) tightly packed fresh flat-leaf parsley leaves

1 pound (450 g) fresh mussels, scrubbed and beards removed

2½ cups (625 mL) Sauvignon Blanc or other unoaked dry white wine

Warm crusty bread, for serving

1. In a large pot, heat the olive oil over medium heat. Add the onion and cook, stirring often, until soft and translucent, about 5 minutes.

2. Add the garlic, lemongrass, salt, and chili flakes. Cook for 30 seconds, stirring constantly. Add the parsley and stir for 30 seconds, until fragrant.

3. Add the mussels, then pour in the wine and stir. Cover with the lid and cook until the mussels open up, about 12 minutes. Remove from the heat. Discard any mussels that did not open.

4. Serve the mussels in bowls with a ladleful of the wine broth. Serve with warm crusty bread.

Tip You can find lemongrass paste in the fresh herb section at the grocery store.

Venetian Seafood Spaghettini

Serves 6

⅔ pound (300 g) spaghettini

¼ cup (60 mL) extra-virgin olive oil

6 cloves garlic, minced

1½ cups (375 mL) tightly packed finely chopped fresh flat-leaf parsley leaves, more for garnish

7 ounces (200 g) medium fresh shrimp, peeled and deveined

7 ounces (200 g) small fresh sea scallops, side muscle removed

7 ounces (200 g) fresh clams, scrubbed

½ teaspoon (2 mL) sea salt

½ teaspoon (2 mL) freshly ground pepper

Pinch of red chili flakes

¾ cup (175 mL) dry white wine

I've always loved pasta dishes with simple sauces. Garlic, olive oil, and a little Parmesan cheese is truly all I need. Every time I visit Venice, I go to a family-owned restaurant away from the busy crowds of San Marco and have the most delicious seafood pasta, plump shrimp and flavourful clams and scallops infusing the spaghettini with all kinds of savoury flavours from the sea, the pasta making me wish I had an Italian nonna to make spaghetti or ravioli with. The comfort of a simple yet satisfying bowl of pasta with seafood is, in my opinion, one of life's most enjoyable pleasures.

This is a great dish to make when friends and family are coming over because it's effortless to prepare, which gives you more time to spend with them, yet it's impressive enough for entertaining. Serve with an arugula salad to transport yourself to the narrow streets of seaside Venice.

1. In a large pot of boiling salted water, cook the spaghettini until just tender, about 11 minutes. Reserve ½ cup (125 mL) of the pasta water, then drain the pasta.

2. Meanwhile, in a large, deep frying pan with a lid, heat the olive oil over medium heat. Add the garlic and parsley and cook, stirring frequently, for 1 minute.

3. Carefully add the shrimp, scallops, and clams. Stir for a few seconds, then season with the salt, pepper, and chili flakes. Pour in the white wine, cover with a lid, and reduce the heat to medium-low. Cook until the clams open, about 8 minutes. Discard any clams that did not open.

4. Using tongs, transfer the pasta to the seafood mixture and stir until all the ingredients are well combined. Sprinkle with parsley and serve.

Zucchini Pasta with Roasted Salmon and Tomatoes

Serves 4

4 tablespoons (60 mL) extra-virgin olive oil, divided

¼ cup (60 mL) fresh lemon juice

2 cloves garlic, finely minced

¼ teaspoon (1 mL) sea salt

¼ teaspoon (1 mL) freshly ground pepper

4 skinless wild salmon fillets (4 ounces/120 g each)

1½ cups (375 mL) cherry tomatoes, cut in half

4 medium zucchini, spiralized

1 cup (250 mL) Garden Pesto (page 69)

Zucchini noodles are a great alternative to pasta, especially during the summer months, when my family craves lighter dinners. I first tried zucchini noodles at a vegetarian restaurant in Barcelona. The noodles were the base for a fresh and nutty pad Thai. It was love at first bite, especially for how the noodles absorbed the sauce and spices of the pad Thai. The first thing I did when I got back to Canada was buy a spiralizer so I could make my own zucchini noodles.

This recipe keeps the zucchini noodles raw—you want them crisp—and coats them in garlicky pesto, then tops them with plump and delicious roasted salmon and tomatoes. This is a perfect meal for busy weeknights, taking less than 40 minutes to prep and cook.

1. Position racks in the upper and lower thirds of the oven. Preheat the oven to 400°F (200°F). Line 2 baking sheets with parchment paper.

2. In a shallow dish large enough to hold the salmon fillets snugly, whisk together 2 tablespoons (30 mL) of the olive oil, the lemon juice, garlic, salt, and pepper. Add the salmon, turn to coat, and let marinate for 10 minutes.

3. Remove the salmon from the marinade and arrange on a prepared baking sheet. Discard the marinade. Slide the baking sheet onto the upper rack of the oven and roast until golden brown, about 18 minutes.

4. Meanwhile, on the other prepared baking sheet, toss the tomatoes with the remaining 2 tablespoons (30 mL) olive oil and a pinch of salt. Slide the baking sheet onto the lower rack and roast until slightly charred, about 8 minutes.

5. Place the zucchini noodles in a large bowl. Spoon in the garden pesto and, using tongs, mix the noodles and pesto until the noodles are well coated.

6. Divide the zucchini noodles among bowls. Top with salmon and tomatoes and serve.

Sesame and Maple Glazed Salmon

Serves 6

⅓ cup (75 mL) tamari

¼ cup (60 mL) extra-virgin olive oil

3 tablespoons (45 mL) sesame oil

2 tablespoons (30 mL) pure maple syrup

5 cloves garlic, finely chopped

1½ teaspoons (7 mL) ginger paste or finely chopped fresh ginger

½ teaspoon (2 mL) sea salt

½ teaspoon (2 mL) freshly ground pepper

1 skinless wild salmon fillet (2 pounds/900 g)

3 green onions (white and light green parts only), finely chopped

1 tablespoon (15 mL) sesame seeds

Toronto has a vibrancy like no other city. It's the place I call home and where I moved to after having lived in Montreal for five years. It's the multicultural food in this "city of neighbourhoods," as Toronto is often called, that makes me love my city so much. You can eat your way through Toronto and find everything under the sun. From Mexican, to Korean, to Ethiopian—every cuisine is represented.

This sesame and maple glazed salmon, inspired by a dish I had at my favourite sushi restaurant, is cooked in our home probably every week. I love serving this delicious staple with roasted sweet potatoes and a green salad. Make sure you top it with lots of green onions and sesame seeds. This salmon also pairs wonderfully with Israeli Couscous with Pistachios, Kalamata Olives, and Goat Cheese (page 175).

1. Preheat the oven to 375°F (190°C). Line a baking sheet with parchment paper or foil.

2. In a medium bowl, whisk together the tamari, olive oil, sesame oil, maple syrup, garlic, ginger, salt, and pepper.

3. Place the salmon in a large baking dish. Pour the tamari mixture over the salmon and let marinate for 15 minutes.

4. Transfer the salmon to the prepared baking sheet. Pour ⅓ cup (75 mL) of the marinade over the salmon. Reserve the remainder of the marinade. Bake the salmon for 25 minutes, or until it flakes easily with a fork.

5. Remove the salmon from the oven and pour the reserved marinade over top. Bake for 3 minutes.

6. Switch the oven to broil. Broil the salmon for 1 minute or until the salmon is golden brown and has a few charred bits. Place the baking sheet on a rack and let the salmon cool for 3 or 4 minutes.

7. Transfer to a platter and just before serving, sprinkle the salmon with the green onions and sesame seeds.

Tip I always have a jar of ginger paste in my fridge to use instead of grating fresh ginger when I'm short on time. It's convenient and yields the same flavour.

Salmon with Shishito Pepper Salad

Serves 2

1 skinless wild salmon fillet
(12 ounces/340 g)
4 tablespoons (60 mL)
extra-virgin olive oil, divided
Juice of 1 lemon
¼ teaspoon (1 mL) sea salt
¼ teaspoon (1 mL) freshly
ground pepper
1 clove garlic, finely minced
2 corn cobs, shucked and each
cut into 4 pieces
12 to 15 shishito peppers,
pierced with a sharp knife
½ teaspoon (2 mL) flaky sea
salt (I use Maldon)
3 vine-ripened tomatoes,
cut in half
½ cup (125 mL) crumbled feta
cheese
1 tablespoon (15 mL) balsamic
vinegar
1 avocado, peeled, pitted, and
sliced
1 teaspoon (5 mL) sesame seeds
⅓ cup (75 mL) Garden Pesto
(page 69)
2 green onions (white and
light green parts only), thinly
sliced on the diagonal
⅓ cup (75 mL) loosely packed
fresh cilantro leaves

I fell in love with shishito peppers on my first trip to Barcelona. A few friends and I walked into one of the tiniest bars I've ever been to. There was not a seat in the house, and barrels served as tables. Busy waiters carrying bottles of chilled cava in one hand and tapas in the other and the sound of glasses and laughter were the best welcome to the city that I am so deeply in love with. That evening, we had *pulpo a la gallega*—a Galician delicacy of thinly sliced braised octopus and potatoes, swimming in a sea of garlicky olive oil—and shrimp croquettes. But it was the shishito peppers that won my heart. Sautéed in olive oil until blistered, and seasoned with flaky sea salt, the peppers were mild in flavour, but one or two on every plate added up to hot.

Back in Toronto I was unable to find them, but the search didn't last long. Bar Raval, my favourite restaurant in the city, served them. Without fail, whenever I visit I order them. One day I came across them at my local grocery store, and on a hot summer day they made it into this savoury salmon salad, full of flavours and spice, and topped with tangy feta and creamy avocado slices.

1. Bring a large pot of water to a boil.

2. Place the salmon in a shallow baking dish. Pour 1 tablespoon (15 mL) of the olive oil and the lemon juice over the salmon. Season with the salt and pepper and sprinkle on the garlic. Let marinate for 10 minutes.

3. Meanwhile, drop the corn into the boiling water and boil for 6 minutes, or until the corn is tender. Remove from the pot and set aside on a plate.

4. In a medium frying pan, heat 1 tablespoon (15 mL) of the olive oil over medium heat. Carefully place the salmon in the pan and cook until the fish has browned and flakes easily with a fork, about 5 minutes per side. Transfer to a large serving board.

continued

5. In another medium frying pan, heat 1 tablespoon (15 mL) of the olive oil over medium heat. Carefully add the peppers and cook until slightly browned and a bit blistered, about 1 minute per side. Using tongs, remove the peppers and arrange them in a mound on the serving board. Sprinkle with the flaky sea salt.

6. In the same frying pan, cook the corn over medium-high heat until all sides are browned a bit, about 1 minute. Using tongs, transfer the corn to the serving board.

7. Arrange the tomatoes in a mound on the serving board. Top the tomatoes with feta cheese. Drizzle the balsamic vinegar and the remaining 1 tablespoon (15 mL) olive oil on top.

8. Arrange the slices of avocado next to the tomatoes and top with the sesame seeds, green onions, and cilantro.

9. Serve with the garden pesto on the side, to drizzle on top if desired.

Tip Shishito peppers are a small and typically mild variety of chili pepper. They are widely used in East Asian cooking as well as in Spain. You can find shishito peppers in the vegetable section at your local grocery store.

Dominican Shrimp and Rice Stew

Serves 8

⅓ pound (170 g) boneless salt
    cod
4 cups (1 L) water
8 Roma tomatoes, cut in half
2 whole cloves garlic + 4 thinly
    sliced cloves garlic, divided
4 tablespoons (60 mL)
    extra-virgin olive oil, divided
1½ teaspoons (7 mL) +
    1 tablespoon (15 mL) sea salt,
    divided
1 large Spanish onion, coarsely
    chopped
2 green onions (white and light
    green parts only), chopped
1 tablespoon + ½ teaspoon
    (17 mL) tomato paste
1½ cups (375 mL) tightly
    packed chopped fresh
    cilantro leaves, divided
8 cups (2 L) vegetable stock
1½ pounds (675 g) large
    shrimp, peeled and deveined
    (shells reserved)
1¼ cups (300 mL) rice (I use
    jasmine)
1 teaspoon (5 mL) freshly
    cracked pepper

For serving
Hot sauce
2 avocados, pitted, peeled,
    and thinly sliced

If there's a meal that reminds me of growing up in Dominican Republic, *asopao de camarones* is it. This flavourful shrimp and rice stew is without a doubt one of my favourite dishes from my beloved birth country. Similar to a shrimp risotto, but soupier in texture, it is usually made on a rainy day, as the temperature drops a few degrees. What makes this dish my favourite? Besides the fact that it reminds me of home, it's pure comfort for the soul. This garlicky tomato-based rice dish can be made with chicken as well, but it is the shrimp and a bit of salt cod that give it such a characteristic flavour. Cilantro is essential to this recipe, but if you're unable to find any, parsley works as well. In true Dominican fashion, make sure you serve it with an ice-cold beer and fried plantains on the side.

Note that you will need to soak the salt cod overnight. This will ensure that the cod is not overly salty.

1. In a large bowl, cover the salt cod with the water. Cover and let sit overnight in the fridge. The next morning, discard the water. Add fresh water and cover. Let sit in the fridge for 1 hour. Remove from the fridge, discard the water again. Add fresh water, cover, and let sit in the fridge for another hour.

2. Preheat the oven to 375°F (190°C). Line a baking sheet with parchment paper.

3. Place the tomatoes and the 2 whole garlic cloves on the prepared baking sheet. Drizzle with 2 tablespoons (30 mL) of the olive oil and sprinkle with ½ teaspoon (2 mL) of the salt. Roast for 15 minutes, or until the tomatoes are slightly browned. Set aside.

4. In a large pot, heat the remaining 2 tablespoons (30 mL) olive oil with 1 teaspoon (5 mL) of the salt over medium heat. Add the sliced garlic and Spanish onion and cook, stirring occasionally, until the onion is soft and translucent, about 5 minutes.

continued

5. Add the green onions and cook, stirring constantly, for 30 seconds. Add the tomato paste and continue to cook, stirring, for 1 minute. Stir in 1 cup (250 mL) of the cilantro. Transfer the onion mixture to the tomato mixture and set aside.

6. In the same pot (no need to wipe clean), combine the vegetable stock, remaining 1 tablespoon (15 mL) salt, and the reserved shrimp shells. Bring to a boil over medium heat. Reduce the heat, cover with a lid, and simmer for 5 minutes. Remove from the heat and discard the shrimp shells.

7. Drain the salt cod and break into large pieces.

8. In a high-speed blender, combine the salt cod, tomato and onion mixture, and half of the shrimp stock. Blend on high speed until smooth.

9. Pour the blended mixture into the remaining shrimp stock and bring to a slow boil. Stir in the rice. Reduce the heat to low, cover with a lid, and cook for 20 minutes, stirring every 5 minutes.

10. Add the shrimp, the remaining ½ cup (125 mL) cilantro, and pepper. Stir for a few seconds. Cover with a lid and cook for 5 minutes.

11. Serve in bowls and enjoy hot with a few dashes of hot sauce. Garnish with avocado slices on top.

Manly Beach Lemongrass Shrimp

Serves 4

1 pound (450 g) large shell-on shrimp, deveined

3 cloves garlic, finely chopped

Juice of 1 lemon

2 tablespoons (30 mL) toasted sesame oil

1 tablespoon (15 mL) lemongrass paste or grated fresh lemongrass (white part only)

¼ teaspoon (1 mL) sea salt

1 cup (250 mL) diced fresh mango

½ cup (125 mL) tightly packed fresh cilantro leaves, more for garnish

2 green onions (white and light green parts only), chopped

2 Thai chili peppers, thinly sliced + 2 whole Thai chili peppers for garnish and more heat (optional)

1 tablespoon (15 mL) extra-virgin olive oil

Sydney, Australia, is a spectacular city. I stayed in Manly Beach, a ferry ride away from Sydney. One night at the pier, I stopped at one of the restaurants facing the water and had the loveliest meal: a salad of edible flowers, pear, and arugula followed by plump shrimp seasoned with lemongrass and a few Thai chilies. The shrimp were grilled to perfection and the aromatic lemongrass was a feast to my senses.

I love recreating dishes from my travels, and this one was no exception. As soon as I got home, I put my own spin on those lemongrass shrimp, adding nutty sesame oil, green onions, and mango to the mix. With just a handful of flavourful ingredients, you'll be able to make one of the most incredible-tasting dishes I've had on my travels. Enjoy with Quinoa Salad with Roasted Vegetables and Feta (page 172) or Arugula, Pear, and Parmesan Salad (page 152.)

1. Place the shrimp in a medium bowl. Add the garlic, lemon juice, sesame oil, lemongrass paste, and salt. Mix to coat the shrimp. Let marinate for 20 minutes.

2. Meanwhile, in a small bowl, combine the mango, cilantro, green onions, and sliced chilies.

3. In a large frying pan, heat the olive oil over medium-high heat. Add the shrimp (discard the marinade), without overcrowding the pan, and cook until the shrimp turn pink, about 2 minutes per side. (You might have to cook the shrimp in 2 batches.)

4. Transfer the cooked shrimp to a platter. Top with the mango salsa. Scatter whole chilies on top, if using.

Tip You can find lemongrass paste next to the fresh herbs in the grocery store. The paste is super-flavourful and eliminates having to peel and grate the lemongrass stalk—a great shortcut on busy days.

Shrimp Stew in Coconut-Tomato Sauce

Serves 6

1 pound (450 g) medium fresh
 shrimp, peeled and deveined

2 tablespoons (30 mL) fresh
 lime juice, divided

3 cloves garlic, finely chopped

1 teaspoon (5 mL) sea salt

3 tablespoons (45 mL) coconut
 oil

1 Spanish onion, thinly sliced

4 green onions (white and
 light green parts only),
 chopped

1 sweet red pepper, thinly
 sliced

½ sweet green pepper, thinly
 sliced

2 teaspoons (10 mL) sweet
 paprika

1 teaspoon (5 mL) red chili
 flakes

3 Roma tomatoes, seeds
 removed, chopped

1 can (14 ounces/400 mL)
 full-fat coconut milk

1 cup (250 mL) loosely packed
 chopped fresh cilantro
 leaves, more for garnish

Steamed jasmine rice, for
 serving

São Paulo, Brazil, is one of the largest cities in South America, and it bustles with culture, art, and a strong food scene. During my visit to this vibrant city, I stopped by a few food markets. I would start my days at the markets with a freshly made mango juice or *maracuya* (passion fruit) juice along with shrimp *moqueca*, an iconic Brazilian dish made by stewing shrimp in a coconut and tomato sauce spiced with sweet peppers, paprika, and a squeeze of lime juice.

At home in Canada, I usually cook this hearty shrimp stew as soon as the temperature starts to drop. It is comforting, filling, and super-satisfying. I also love that most of the ingredients can be found in my fridge and pantry, making this stew a breeze to pull together for dinner.

1. In a medium bowl, toss the shrimp with 1 tablespoon (15 mL) of the lime juice, 1 tablespoon (15 mL) of the chopped garlic, and the salt. Let marinate for 20 minutes.

2. Meanwhile, in a large pot, melt the coconut oil over medium-high heat. Add the Spanish onion and green onions and cook, stirring often, until the onions are soft and translucent, about 5 minutes. Add the red pepper, green pepper, paprika, chili flakes, and the remaining garlic and cook, stirring constantly, for 30 seconds.

3. Reduce the heat to medium. Add the tomatoes, coconut milk, and a pinch of salt. Cook, stirring occasionally, for 10 minutes, or until the sauce reduces and thickens a bit.

4. Add the shrimp with the marinade and the remaining 1 tablespoon (15 mL) lime juice. Gently simmer until the shrimp turn pink, about 3 minutes. Stir in the cilantro. Serve over steamed rice, garnished with cilantro.

North Shore Shrimp

Serves 4

The drive from Waikiki to the North Shore of Hawaii is one of those trips that needs to be experienced at least once in a lifetime. Endless miles of pristine beaches, deep turquoise waters under the sun, and my favourite thing of all, food trucks all along the way. With my first taste of North Shore shrimp from one of those food trucks, I fell madly in love with this delicious dish. Since then, I often make it at home, not only because I love its garlicky and lemony flavour, but because I'm all about simple weekday meals that take little time to make but don't compromise on taste. The velvety sauce that the shrimp cooks in can easily be used with any other fish as well.

¾ cup (175 mL) all-purpose flour

1½ teaspoons (7 mL) sweet paprika

1½ teaspoons (7 mL) sea salt, divided

1 pound (450 g) large fresh shrimp, peeled and deveined

3 tablespoons (45 mL) canola oil

8 cloves garlic, coarsely chopped

½ cup (125 mL) dry white wine

3 tablespoons (45 mL) unsalted butter

½ cup (125 mL) tightly packed chopped fresh cilantro leaves, more for garnish

4 teaspoons (20 mL) fresh lemon juice

Steamed jasmine rice, for serving

1. In a shallow bowl, stir together the flour, paprika, and 1 teaspoon (5 mL) of the salt. Lightly dredge the shrimp in the flour mixture, shaking off any excess flour. Transfer to a plate and set aside.

2. In a large frying pan, heat the canola oil over medium-low heat. Add the garlic and the remaining ½ teaspoon (2 mL) salt. Cook, stirring constantly, until the garlic is slightly golden, about 2 minutes. Using a slotted spoon, remove the garlic and set aside.

3. Increase the heat to medium-high. Add the shrimp in a single layer and cook for 2 minutes (you may need to cook the shrimp in 2 batches). Turn the shrimp and cook for another 2 minutes, or until the shrimp turn pink and opaque.

4. Add the white wine and continue to cook for 2 minutes, or until the liquid has reduced by half.

5. Add the butter and the reserved garlic. Cook, stirring often, until the butter has melted and the sauce looks a bit thick, about 3 minutes.

6. Remove from the heat, stir in the cilantro and lemon juice, and toss to combine. Serve with steamed rice.

Shrimp Tacos with Chipotle Crema

Serves 4

1 pound (450 g) fresh or
thawed frozen medium
shrimp, peeled and deveined

¼ cup (60 mL) + 2 tablespoons
(30 mL) lemon juice, divided

4 tablespoons (60 mL)
extra-virgin olive oil, divided

½ teaspoon (2 mL) chipotle
chili powder

¼ teaspoon (1 mL) sea salt

1 clove garlic, finely minced

1 cup (250 mL) full-fat sour
cream

2 tablespoons (30 mL) finely
chopped chipotle peppers in
adobo sauce

8 corn tortillas

2½ cups (625 mL) finely
shredded purple cabbage

2 avocados, peeled, pitted, and
sliced

1 cup (250 mL) crumbled feta
cheese

1 cup (250 mL) tightly packed
fresh cilantro leaves

4 green onions (white and
light green parts only), thinly
sliced

½ lemon, for serving (optional)

If I had to name my family's most requested dish, it would be shrimp tacos. For them, there's nothing better than corn tortillas topped with chipotle-marinated shrimp, crunchy purple cabbage, slices of creamy avocado, and a simple chipotle crema. Years spent living in Mexico City gave me a deep appreciation for Mexican cuisine, and later I discovered that it can be found in almost every country in the world. Walk into one of the many taquerias in Los Angeles or Sydney, Australia, and shrimp tacos will be on the menu. In Toronto, we are lucky to have a few restaurants that make some of the best Mexican food around. You can bet that when I stop for a bite at one of these restaurants, I'll be ordering shrimp tacos. The smell of the corn tortillas takes me back to living in a country that has one of the richest food scenes in the world.

1. In a large bowl, combine the shrimp, ¼ cup (60 mL) of the lemon juice, 2 tablespoons (30 mL) of the olive oil, chili powder, salt, and garlic. Give it a stir to fully coat the shrimp with the marinade. Let marinate for 10 minutes.

2. In a medium bowl, whisk together the sour cream, the remaining 2 tablespoons (30 mL) lemon juice, and the chipotle peppers until the mixture turns a light pinkish colour. Set aside the chipotle crema.

3. In a large frying pan, heat the remaining 2 tablespoons (30 mL) olive oil over medium heat. Add the shrimp, without overcrowding the pan. (You might have to cook the shrimp in 2 batches.) Cook for 2 minutes per side, until the shrimp turn pink. Transfer the shrimp to a plate. Wipe the pan clean.

4. In the same pan, heat the tortillas over medium heat for 1 minute per side, or until heated through.

5. To assemble, spread 2 tablespoons (30 mL) of the chipotle crema over each tortilla. Top with 4 or 5 shrimp, cabbage, a few slices of avocado, 1 tablespoon (15 mL) feta, a few cilantro leaves, and a sprinkle of green onions. Squeeze lemon juice over the tacos, if using.

Piri-Piri Roasted Fish

Serves 4

4 skinless tilapia or halibut fillets (4 ounces/115 g each)

3 cups (750 mL) halved new potatoes or fingerling potatoes

1½ sweet red peppers, thinly sliced

1 large red onion, thinly sliced

Juice of 1½ lemons, more for serving (optional)

4 cloves garlic, thinly sliced

⅓ cup (75 mL) extra-virgin olive oil

1 tablespoon (15 mL) piri-piri powder

½ teaspoon (2 mL) sea salt

½ cup (125 mL) tightly packed chopped fresh flat-leaf parsley leaves

2 green onions (white and light green parts only), thinly sliced

Lisbon is such a spectacular city. Over the years, I've had the chance to visit several times, and each time I love it even more. How not to love its beautiful views, so easily admired from the many *miradores*, or lookout points, located throughout the city? But if I had to choose what makes this city so special to me, it is definitely its food and spices.

When I'm in Lisbon, I always buy piri-piri powder to bring back home and add to seafood and vegetable dishes. This piri-piri roasted fish couldn't be any easier to make—a sheet pan meal that is ideal for busy nights and is loaded with zesty and peppery flavours. Tender fish fillets, hearty potatoes, and sweet peppers marinated and baked in the tastiest (and most garlicky) piri-piri sauce. Enjoy with a chilled glass of Portuguese vinho verde!

1. Preheat the oven to 375°F (190 C). Line a baking sheet with parchment paper.

2. Place the fish on the prepared baking sheet. Scatter the potatoes, red peppers, and red onion around the fish.

3. In a small bowl, whisk together the lemon juice, garlic, olive oil, piri-piri, and salt until there are no lumps and the marinade is smooth. Pour over the fish and vegetables and let marinate for 15 minutes.

4. Roast for 18 minutes, rotating the pan halfway through.

5. Set the oven to broil. Broil for 1 minute, or until the fish is golden brown on top.

6. To serve, sprinkle parsley and green onions over the fish. Sprinkle with a little lemon juice, if using.

Summer Halibut with Nectarine Salsa and Roasted Asparagus

Serves 2

The cuisine in Vancouver is chock full of delicious seafood. In my many visits to this fantastic city, I make it a point to go to one of my favourite restaurants, Chambar, where I know the fish of the day will come cooked to perfection and probably topped with a fresh salsa. This recipe is inspired by the beauty and suppleness of the West Coast food scene, where the flavours are always delightfully bold. For a true taste of summer, serve a green salad on the side.

Nectarine Salsa

2 nectarines, peeled and sliced

1 plum, sliced

⅓ cup (75 mL) loosely packed fresh mint leaves

2 tablespoons (30 mL) extra-virgin olive oil

2 tablespoons (30 mL) dry white wine

Summer Halibut

2 skinless halibut fillets (8 ounces/225 g each)

4 tablespoons (60 mL) extra-virgin olive oil, divided

3 tablespoons (45 mL) fresh lemon juice

1½ teaspoons (7 mL) tamari

2 cloves garlic, finely minced

¼ teaspoon (1 mL) sea salt

¼ teaspoon (1 mL) pepper

Roasted Asparagus

8 asparagus spears, trimmed

2 tablespoons (30 mL) balsamic vinegar

1 tablespoon (15 mL) sesame oil

1. To make the nectarine salsa: In a medium bowl, combine the nectarines, plum, mint, olive oil, and white wine. Stir well and set aside.

2. Position the racks in the upper and lower thirds of the oven. Preheat the oven to 375°F (190°C). Line a baking sheet with parchment paper.

3. To make the summer halibut: Cut each fillet crosswise into 3 equal portions, each about 2 inches (5 cm) wide. Place the fish in a shallow baking dish. Drizzle 2 tablespoons (30 mL) of the olive oil, the lemon juice, and tamari over the fish. Sprinkle with the garlic, salt, and pepper. Let marinate for 10 minutes.

4. In a medium oven-safe frying pan, heat the remaining 2 tablespoons (30 mL) olive oil over medium-high heat. Add the fish and sear for 2 minutes per side. Transfer the pan to the lower rack in the oven and roast the fish until golden brown, about 15 minutes.

5. Meanwhile, to roast the asparagus: Arrange the asparagus on the prepared baking sheet. Drizzle with the balsamic vinegar and sesame oil. Transfer the baking sheet to the upper rack in the oven and roast the asparagus until tender, about 8 minutes.

6. Serve the halibut with the nectarine salsa and the roasted asparagus.

Garlic Cod with Thyme Lentils and Roasted Carrots

Serves 4

There's nowhere else I would rather eat cod than in Lisbon. Walk into any restaurant in the city and you'll find it on the menu. In the neighbourhood of Alfama, I enjoyed it with eggplant, potatoes, and chickpeas, while in nearby Bairro Alto, it was served over polenta cooked in cream and rosemary. At home, my favourite way to cook cod is to roast it in the oven with lots of garlic. This gives the fish a wonderful golden crust while keeping it moist inside. In this recipe I serve it over thyme-scented lentils alongside carrots roasted with a little orange juice. This dish is deeply comforting, very simple to make, nutritious, and perfect for a cozy dinner at home.

3½ cups (875 mL) vegetable stock

1½ cups (375 mL) dried brown lentils, rinsed and drained

4 sprigs fresh thyme

1 tablespoon (15 mL) + 1½ teaspoons (7 mL) sea salt, divided

16 small carrots, peeled

¼ cup (60 mL) fresh orange juice

¼ cup (60 mL) + 3 tablespoons (45 mL) extra-virgin olive oil, divided

4 skinless cod fillets (9 ounces/255 g each)

Juice of 1 lemon

4 cloves garlic, finely minced

1 teaspoon (5 mL) freshly cracked pepper

½ lemon, for serving (optional)

1. In a large saucepan, bring the vegetable stock to a boil. Add the lentils, thyme, and 1 tablespoon (15 mL) of the salt. Cook, covered with a lid, over medium-low heat until the lentils are tender, 35 to 40 minutes. Drain, discard the thyme sprigs, and set aside, keeping warm.

2. Preheat the oven to 400°F (200°C). Line a baking sheet with parchment paper.

3. On the prepared baking sheet, toss the carrots with the orange juice and 1 tablespoon (15 mL) of the olive oil. Roast for 15 minutes, turning once, until fork-tender and golden brown.

4. Meanwhile, place the cod fillets in a large, shallow baking dish. Pour ¼ cup (60 mL) of the olive oil and the lemon juice over the fish. Sprinkle with the garlic, the remaining 1½ teaspoons (7 mL) salt, and pepper. Let marinate for 10 minutes.

5. In a large frying pan, heat the remaining 2 tablespoons (30 mL) olive oil. Carefully place the fish fillets in the pan and cook until the fish is light golden and flakes with a fork, about 4 minutes per side.

6. To serve, place 1 cup (250 mL) of the lentils on each plate. Top with a piece of cod and 4 carrots. Squeeze a little lemon juice over the fish, if using.

Samaná Coconut Tilapia

Serves 4

Samaná is a city in the eastern part of Dominican Republic famous for its rich fishing culture and abundant seafood and fish recipes. One of my favourite dishes from back home is a pan-fried fish topped with the most delicious but simple creamy coconut-tomato sauce. I've been cooking this recipe ever since I moved to Canada, and it automatically brings back memories of growing up in my sunny island, where my mom and stepdad would make it for me on weekends. The tilapia cooks in the flavourful coconut-tomato sauce and is wonderful with jasmine rice on the side.

Tilapia

4 skinless tilapia fillets
(6 ounces/170 g each)
2 cloves garlic, finely minced
3 tablespoons (45 mL)
extra-virgin olive oil, divided
Juice of 1 lemon
¼ teaspoon (1 mL) dried
oregano
¼ teaspoon (1 mL) sea salt
¼ teaspoon (1 mL) freshly
ground pepper

Coconut-Tomato Sauce

2 tablespoons (30 mL)
extra-virgin olive oil
1 medium Spanish onion,
chopped
2 cloves garlic, finely minced
2 green onions (white and
light green parts only), thinly
sliced, more for garnish
2 tablespoons (30 mL) tomato
paste
1 can (14 ounces /400 mL)
full-fat coconut milk
1 cup (250 mL) tightly packed
fresh cilantro leaves, more
for serving
Steamed jasmine rice, for
serving

1. To prepare the tilapia: Place the fish in a baking dish large enough to accommodate the 4 fillets. Sprinkle with the garlic. Pour 1 tablespoon (15 mL) of the olive oil and the lemon juice over the fish. Season with oregano, salt, and pepper. Let marinate for 10 minutes.

2. To make the coconut-tomato sauce: In a medium saucepan, heat the olive oil over medium heat. Add the Spanish onion and cook, stirring often, until soft and translucent, about 5 minutes.

3. Add the garlic and cook for 30 seconds, stirring often. Stir in the green onions and tomato paste and cook for 1 minute.

4. Stir in the coconut milk and cilantro. Cover with the lid, reduce the heat to low, and simmer, stirring occasionally, for 8 minutes.

5. Meanwhile, cook the fish: In a large frying pan, heat the remaining 2 tablespoons (30 mL) olive oil over medium heat. Carefully place the fish in the pan, discarding the marinade. Cook until golden brown, about 4 minutes per side.

6. Pour the coconut-tomato sauce over the fish. Cook for 2 minutes.

7. Serve the fish topped with a sprinkle of green onions, some cilantro, and rice on the side.

San Francisco

From the beginning of my journey into cooking, two restaurants always came to mind: Zuni Café and Chez Panisse. For years these two quintessential restaurants have captured the true soul of California cuisine. Alice Waters poured her whole being into Chez Panisse, elevating farm-to-table cuisine with an undying commitment to the Slow Food movement, working with farmers, foragers, and purveyors. Both restaurants published cookbooks that instantly found a home in my kitchen, becoming my inspiration for Sunday meals. From Zuni's I revered the citrus risotto and the lentil–sweet red pepper soup. I would gather fruit to bake Chez Panisse's apricot bread pudding and fragrant pear crisp. I knew that someday a trip to California was in order, especially to San Francisco.

It was not until years later that I would find myself in this beautiful city with my dear friend Amy and both of our daughters. We explored the Mission District's food scene while making stops at flower markets and enjoying the lushness of Dolores Park. People soaking up the sun laid out their picnics on colourful blankets. I spotted baskets carrying cheeses, juicy grapes, and crusty breads. While live music played and someone blew giant bubbles across the park, we marvelled at a clear view of downtown San Francisco. It didn't take us long to love this city's buoyancy.

I plan most of my travels around food, and starting our days in San Francisco called for an early-morning visit to Tartine Bakery, a mecca of all things bread and pastry. The hype about this iconic bakery was real, and that day Tartine was the definition of pastry paradise in my books. Taking the first bite of the most flaky and buttery croissant brought back memories of the many trays I had baked in pastry school; Tartine's are simply unparalleled. We were like kids in a candy store, and we chose morning buns, a delightful asparagus tartine, strawberry tarts filled with the most delicate pastry cream speckled with vanilla seeds, as well as croissants and pains au chocolat. We left Tartine happy, grateful, and vowing to come back soon.

After breakfast and on our way to winding Lombard Street, I couldn't help but think that one of the things I love the most about travel is landing in a new city and discovering it through its food. Trying meals across this city, from the Mission to Nob Hill, from the Fillmore to the Marina, I marvelled at the diversity: it seemed every culture was represented in food. Spots like La Taqueria, Delfina pizzeria, and Mission Chinese Food come to mind.

San Francisco took my breath away, and I can't wait to go back and keep exploring its many neighbourhoods with their jaw-dropping views, fantastic food, and always colourful bougainvillea.

Desserts

My love for desserts started when I was a child, when after my piano lessons my mother would take me for chocolate cake at this little ice cream parlour that was famous for its thick and delicious milkshakes. I still remember how the buttercream frosting was velvety smooth and how the cake had hints of Dominican vanilla that gave it such a wonderful fragrance. Years later, when I moved to Canada and started collecting cookbooks, I would spend hours in the kitchen. Most of my cookbooks were about baking, so I started with simple cookies, fruit cobblers, and loaves. Then it was time to learn the art of pastry. I took on apple-caramel and strawberry pies, lemon tarts, and three-layer cakes that I would carefully frost with glossy Italian buttercream speckled with vanilla. Baking became a way of showing love, and still today, time spent making desserts not only brings me joy but leaves me with a sense of calm that I treasure.

Later in life, I had the chance to make a big dream come true. While living in Mexico City for three years, I attended Le Cordon Bleu. From early morning till evening, four days a week, I would spend hours learning how to make flaky puff pastry, tray after tray of buttery croissants, macarons that our *pâtissier* made us make over again and again until they were perfect. Opera cake, hazelnut mille-feuille, bûche de Noël, and croquembouche. It was heaven! I would return home with all the treats I'd made that day to share with my family.

Since then, all my travels around the world involve stopping at bakeries and trying local desserts that inspire me once I'm back home. Throughout the years I've gathered a repertoire of favourites that celebrate family and special occasions that I am thrilled to share with you. Whether Pumpkin Scones with Maple Cinnamon Glaze (page 227), Coconut Flan (page 241), or Spanish Custard (page 239), these desserts are my family's favourites and I hope they soon become yours as well.

Caramelized Banana and Cinnamon Loaf

Makes 1 loaf, Serves 12

1½ cups (375 mL) all-purpose flour

¼ cup (60 mL) whole wheat flour

1 tablespoon (15 mL) chia seeds

1 tablespoon (15 mL) hemp hearts

1½ teaspoons (7 mL) baking soda

1½ teaspoons (7 mL) cinnamon

¾ teaspoon (4 mL) sea salt

3 eggs

1½ cups (375 mL) granulated sugar

1 cup mashed bananas (about 2 very ripe large bananas)

¾ cup (175 mL) vegetable oil

2 tablespoons (30 mL) plain full-fat Greek yogurt

2 teaspoons (10 mL) pure vanilla extract

1 very ripe banana, cut into 3 lengthwise slices (each about ¼ inch/5 mm thick)

1 tablespoon (15 mL) unsalted butter, melted

Once when I was strolling through the SoHo district of New York City, I stumbled upon a bakery I had been wanting to visit for years. Their approach to baking was uncomplicated. Peanut butter cookies and chocolate chip cookies were their best sellers, but I felt drawn to a perfectly golden-brown loaf of banana cake. It was deliciously specked with walnuts and, to my surprise, spiced with Ceylon cinnamon. This caramelized banana and cinnamon loaf is the one I make the most at home, especially in autumn or when I have ripe bananas to use up. I love adding chia seeds and hemp hearts for a boost of nutrition. A warm slice goes perfectly with a hot cup of chai.

1. Position a rack in the middle of the oven. Preheat the oven to 350°F (180°C). Grease a 9- × 5-inch (2 L) loaf pan with nonstick spray.

2. In a medium bowl, whisk together the all-purpose flour, whole wheat flour, chia seeds, hemp hearts, baking soda, cinnamon, and salt.

3. In a large bowl, whisk together the eggs, sugar, mashed bananas, vegetable oil, yogurt, and vanilla.

4. Add the flour mixture to the banana mixture and stir to combine. Do not overmix. A few specks of flour in the batter is okay.

5. Scrape the batter into the prepared pan and smooth the top. Arrange the 3 banana slices on top. Brush the butter over the batter. Bake for 60 to 65 minutes, until a toothpick inserted in the centre of the loaf comes out clean. Transfer to a rack and let the loaf cool in the pan for 12 minutes.

6. Run a knife around the inside of the pan to release the loaf. Turn out the loaf onto the rack and let cool completely before serving. Store in a covered container at room temperature for up to 3 days or in the freezer for up to 1 month.

Blueberry and Tangerine Scones

Makes 8 scones

My introduction to scones was in New York City while visiting my godmother. I was in my teens, and my mother and I would often spend a few weeks in the city that never sleeps and that happens to have lots of bakeries. After dinner, we would walk around Greenwich Village and pick up a few treats for breakfast that somehow wouldn't last till breakfast. I still love scones, and at home I serve them not only at breakfast but often as a dessert as well.

These blueberry and tangerine scones are made with cream and the zest of fragrant tangerines that makes them taste light and fresh.

2 cups (500 mL) all-purpose flour

3 tablespoons (45 mL) granulated sugar

1 tablespoon (15 mL) baking powder

¾ teaspoon (4 mL) sea salt

6 tablespoons (90 mL) cold unsalted butter, cut into pieces

1½ cups (375 mL) fresh blueberries, rinsed and patted dry

1 tablespoon (15 mL) tangerine or clementine zest

2 eggs, lightly beaten

⅓ cup (75 mL) whipping (35%) cream, more for brushing

1 teaspoon (5 mL) pure vanilla extract

3 tablespoons (45 mL) turbinado sugar

1. Position a rack in the middle of the oven. Preheat the oven to 400°F (200°C). Line a baking sheet with parchment paper.

2. In a large bowl, sift together the flour, granulated sugar, baking powder, and salt. Using a pastry cutter, cut in the butter until it's the size of peas. Stir in the blueberries and tangerine zest.

3. In a medium bowl, whisk together the eggs, cream, and vanilla. Make a well in the centre of the flour mixture and pour the cream mixture into the well. Stir with a fork just until combined. A few crumbly pieces are okay.

4. Turn out the dough onto a lightly floured work surface and shape it into a 6-inch (15 cm) square about 1¼ inches (3 cm) thick. Using a sharp floured knife or bench scraper, cut the dough into quarters, then cut each quarter into 2 triangles.

5. Transfer the scones to the prepared baking sheet. Lightly brush the tops with cream and sprinkle with turbinado sugar. Bake for 20 to 22 minutes, until golden brown.

6. Transfer the scones to a rack and let cool for 8 to 10 minutes before serving. Store in a covered container at room temperature for up to 3 days or in the freezer for up to 1 month. If serving from frozen, thaw, then reheat in the oven at 300°F (150°C) for 4 minutes.

Tip If clementines or tangerines are not in season, feel free to use orange zest instead.

Pumpkin Scones with Maple Cinnamon Glaze

Makes 8 scones

Pumpkin Scones

2 cups (500 mL) all-purpose
  flour

½ cup (125 mL) granulated
  sugar

2 teaspoons (10 mL) baking
  powder

1 teaspoon (5 mL) cinnamon

½ teaspoon (2 mL) ground
  ginger

½ teaspoon (2 mL) nutmeg

½ teaspoon (2 mL) sea salt

¼ teaspoon (1 mL) baking
  soda

¾ cup (175 mL/165 g) cold
  unsalted butter (1½ sticks)

½ cup (125 mL) raw pecans,
  chopped

1 egg

½ cup + 1 tablespoon (140 mL)
  canned pure pumpkin purée

¼ cup (60 mL) cold
  buttermilk, well shaken

1½ teaspoons (7 mL) pure
  vanilla extract

⅓ cup (75 mL) cold whipping
  (35%) cream

2 tablespoons (30 mL)
  turbinado sugar

The neighbourhood of Westmount in Montreal was home for most of the years I lived in the city. Filled with bakeries and gourmet grocery shops, this is where I first got into baking. I would walk to a nearby grocery store, Les 5 Saisons, and come home with bags filled with Valrhona chocolate, Tahitian vanilla, and other ingredients to bake cookies, flans, and cakes. My love for baking grew more when I discovered the nearby Atwater Market, a paradise that showcases seasonal ingredients from all over Quebec. I particularly loved it during autumn, when pumpkins in all their glorious splendour adorned every corner of the market.

These fragrantly spiced pumpkin scones are buttery yet crisp on top, tender inside, and not overly sweet. Topped with a creamy maple cinnamon glaze, they are autumn in a triangle. A sweet homage to Montreal—my first home in Canada.

1. Line a baking sheet with parchment paper.

2. To make the pumpkin scones: In a large bowl, sift together the flour, granulated sugar, baking powder, cinnamon, ginger, nutmeg, salt, and baking soda. Using the large holes of a box grater, grate the butter over the flour mixture. Gently toss the butter into the flour mixture to evenly distribute it. Stir in the chopped pecans.

3. In another large bowl, whisk together the egg, pumpkin purée, buttermilk, and vanilla.

4. Pour the buttermilk mixture into the flour mixture and stir with a wooden spoon until just combined. Be careful not to overmix. The dough will look slightly crumbly.

5. Transfer the dough to a lightly floured work surface. Shape into a disc 1½ inches (4 cm) thick. Using a sharp floured knife or bench scraper, cut the disc into 8 wedges. Transfer the scones to the prepared baking sheet and freeze for 30 minutes, until firm.

6. Meanwhile, position a rack in the middle of the oven. Preheat the oven to 400°F (200°C).

continued

Maple Cinnamon Glaze

2 cups (500 mL) icing sugar

1 tablespoon (15 mL) cinnamon

½ teaspoon (2 mL) sea salt

½ cup (125 mL) pure maple syrup

2 tablespoons (30 mL) unsalted butter, melted

1 teaspoon (5 mL) pure vanilla extract

½ cup (125 mL) raw pepitas, toasted

7. Remove the scones from the freezer, brush the tops with the cream, and sprinkle with the turbinado sugar. Bake until golden brown, 25 to 28 minutes. Transfer to a rack to cool for 10 minutes.

8. Meanwhile, make the maple cinnamon glaze: In a medium bowl, whisk together the icing sugar, cinnamon, and salt. Pour in the maple syrup, melted butter, and vanilla. Whisk together until the glaze is completely smooth.

9. Once the scones have cooled for 10 minutes, spread 2 tablespoons (30 mL) of the glaze on top of each scone. Sprinkle with toasted pepitas. The scones are best the day they are made, but can be stored in a covered container at room temperature for up to 2 days or in the freezer (without the glaze and toasted pepitas) for up to 1 month.

Summer Berry Galette

Serves 6

Pastry

1¼ cups (300 mL) all-purpose
flour

1 tablespoon (15 mL)
granulated sugar

¼ teaspoon (1 mL) sea salt

8 tablespoons (125 mL/110 g)
cold unsalted butter (1 stick),
cubed

4 teaspoons (20 mL) ice water

1 tablespoon (15 mL) fresh
lemon juice

Berry Filling

½ cup (125 mL) firmly packed
brown sugar

3 tablespoons (45 mL)
cornstarch

⅛ teaspoon (0.5 mL) sea salt

4 cups (1 L) mixed fresh berries
(such as strawberries cut in
half, blueberries, raspberries,
blackberries)

1 tablespoon (15 mL) turbinado
sugar

4 teaspoons (20 mL) pure
maple syrup

Vanilla ice cream, for serving

A summer doesn't go by without my baking several galettes. All the farmers' markets around where I live are filled with baskets of the most fragrant berries, plump cherries, and juicy peaches. After my weekly trip to the market, my kitchen counters are topped with all kinds of fruits, and a galette definitely needs to be made. Galettes are extremely easy to make, and for those who are not quite ready to crimp a pie, a galette is the perfect option. In my travels I've tried all kinds of galettes, from pear and almond to plum and pistachio, but it is this simple summer berry recipe that I make every summer to celebrate the fruitful bounty of the season in the Niagara region of Ontario, where I live.

The pastry dough can be made up to three days ahead. Wrap in plastic wrap and store in the fridge until ready to use. Let sit at room temperature for 20 to 25 minutes before rolling out. You can use any mix of fruit, such as peaches, berries, plums, apples, and apricots.

1. Position a rack in the middle of the oven. Preheat the oven to 375°F (190°C).

2. To make the pastry: In a food processor, combine the flour, granulated sugar, and salt. Pulse to mix. Add the butter and pulse until the butter is the size of peas. With the motor running, pour in the ice water and lemon juice, and continue to pulse just until the dough comes together in a loose ball. It should not be sticky. If it is, pulse in 1 teaspoon (5 mL) flour.

3. Lay a large piece of parchment paper on the counter and sprinkle lightly with flour. Scrape out the dough and shape into a ball. Using a lightly floured rolling pin, roll the dough into a 12-inch (30 cm) circle. The pastry will be thin and the edges will be uneven. Carefully slide the parchment paper with the pastry onto a baking sheet.

continued

4. To make the berry filling: In a large bowl, stir together the brown sugar, cornstarch, and salt. Gently stir in the berries until coated. Transfer the fruit mixture to the middle of the pastry circle and level it out, leaving a 2-inch (5 cm) border. Fold the pastry border up over the filling, pleating where needed.

5. Lightly brush the pastry with water, then sprinkle with the turbinado sugar. Bake until the crust is golden brown and the filling is bubbly, 35 to 40 minutes. Transfer the baking sheet to a rack and let cool for 10 minutes before serving. Brush the fruit filling with maple syrup. Serve warm with a scoop of vanilla ice cream.

Niagara Fruit Crisp

Fruit Crisp

2 cups (500 mL) fresh
blueberries

2 cups (500 mL) fresh
strawberries

2 cups (500 mL) fresh
raspberries

3 tablespoons (45 mL) orange
liqueur

⅓ cup + 2 tablespoons
(105 mL) granulated sugar

¼ cup (60 mL) all-purpose
flour

¼ teaspoon (1 mL) cinnamon

Oat Topping

1 cup (250 mL) large-flake
rolled oats

½ cup (125 mL) all-purpose
flour

½ cup (125 mL) firmly packed
brown sugar

½ cup (125 mL) granulated
sugar

⅛ teaspoon (0.5 mL) sea salt

½ cup (125 mL/110 g) cold
unsalted butter (1 stick), cut
into pieces

For serving

Sliced raw almonds, toasted

Vanilla ice cream or whipped
cream

At a Portuguese bakery in New York City, I had a summer fruit crisp infused with port. The juiciest cherries and berries were softened into a syrupy jam that was lightly topped with a cinnamony nut and oat streusel. The crisp was warm out of the oven and served with vanilla ice cream that slowly melted on top. It was one luscious treat.

The simplicity of fruit crisp is what inspires me to bake a few each summer. The farmers' markets near where I live have an abundance of juicy local peaches, sweet and plump berries, and local cherries that are perfect for baking with. Serve this fruit crisp with vanilla ice cream or freshly whipped cream.

1. Position a rack in the middle of the oven. Preheat the oven to 350°F (180°C). Butter a 13- × 9-inch (3 L) baking dish.

2. To make the fruit crisp: In a large bowl, combine the blueberries, strawberries, and raspberries with the orange liqueur, granulated sugar, flour, and cinnamon. Stir gently to mix. Carefully tip the mixture into the prepared baking dish.

3. To make the oat topping: In a medium bowl, combine the oats, flour, brown sugar, granulated sugar, and salt. Using a pastry blender, cut in the butter until the mixture resembles a coarse meal. Sprinkle the oat mixture evenly over the fruit mixture.

4. Bake until the fruit is bubbling and the topping is golden brown, 50 to 55 minutes. Let cool slightly on a rack before serving.

5. Serve warm with a sprinkle of almonds and a scoop of vanilla ice cream or a dollop of whipped cream.

Farmers' Market Cobbler

Serves 8

Fruit Filling

8 cups (2 L) sliced very ripe
  fresh peaches (15 to
  16 medium peaches)

1½ cups (375 mL) fresh
  blueberries

⅓ cup (75 mL) granulated
  sugar

3 tablespoons (45 mL)
  cornstarch

2 tablespoons (30 mL) firmly
  packed light brown sugar

½ teaspoon (2 mL) lemon zest

1 tablespoon (15 mL) fresh
  lemon juice

Biscuit Topping

2 cups (500 mL) all-purpose
  flour

⅓ cup (75 mL) granulated
  sugar

2 teaspoons (10 mL) baking
  powder

¼ teaspoon (1 mL) sea salt

8 tablespoons (125 mL/110 g)
  cold unsalted butter (1 stick),
  cut into pieces

1 cup (250 mL) + 2 tablespoons
  (30 mL) whipping (35%)
  cream, divided

1 teaspoon (5 mL) pure vanilla
  extract

2 tablespoons (30 mL)
  turbinado sugar

Vanilla ice cream, for serving

August in the Niagara region of Ontario, where I live, is the perfect time to pick your own peaches at many of the farms. The farmers' markets have ripe and juicy peaches and berries that make baking one of my favourite things to do during the summer. For this cobbler, use the ripest peaches you can find. They will turn into a jammy sauce that will be fragrantly topped with a fluffy layer of buttery vanilla biscuits. Enjoy with a scoop of your favourite vanilla ice cream.

1. Position a rack in the middle of the oven. Preheat the oven to 375°F (190°C). Line a baking sheet with parchment paper.

2. To prepare the fruit filling: In a large bowl, combine the peaches, blueberries, granulated sugar, cornstarch, brown sugar, lemon zest, and lemon juice. Stir gently to mix. Spoon the mixture into a 13- × 9-inch (3 L) baking dish; set aside.

3. To make the biscuit topping: In a medium bowl, whisk together the flour, granulated sugar, baking powder, and salt. Using a pastry blender or 2 knives, cut in the butter until the pieces are the size of peas.

4. In a small bowl, stir together 1 cup (250 mL) of the cream and the vanilla. Pour the cream mixture into the flour mixture and stir until a soft and sticky dough forms.

5. Divide the dough into 8 equal pieces (about 2 heaping tablespoons/36 mL each) and spoon them evenly over the fruit filling. Brush the dough with the remaining 2 tablespoons (30 mL) cream and sprinkle the turbinado sugar on top.

6. Place the baking dish on the prepared baking sheet and bake until the juices are bubbling and the topping is golden brown, 55 to 65 minutes. If the topping browns too quickly, cover with foil. Let cool on a rack for 30 minutes before serving. Serve warm with a scoop of vanilla ice cream.

Cherry and Almond Clafoutis

Serves 8

3 eggs

1 cup (250 mL) whole milk

½ cup (125 mL) plain full-fat Greek yogurt

⅓ cup (75 mL) granulated sugar

½ cup (125 mL) all-purpose flour

½ teaspoon (2 mL) sea salt

1 teaspoon (5 mL) pure almond extract

4 tablespoons (60 mL/55 g) unsalted butter (½ stick), melted

Zest of ½ lemon

1 cup (250 mL) pitted fresh sweet cherries

¼ cup (60 mL) icing sugar, for dusting

Toasted sliced raw almonds, for serving (optional)

I was in a French bakery in Montreal the first time I tried cherry clafoutis. Immediately I was intrigued by this warm and custardy dessert with subtle hints of almond. The cherries were juicy, and their tartness balanced the sweetness of the custard. The owner mentioned that he also baked clafoutis with plums and another with apricots and Grand Marnier. The following week I went back and tried them both. Since then, clafoutis has become a staple at home—a dessert that I can have ready in under an hour and surprise my family with after dinner. My daughters prefer cherry in the summer, but come winter, my favourite is apple and pear with a dusting of toasted almonds.

1. In a medium bowl, combine the eggs, milk, yogurt, granulated sugar, flour, salt, and almond extract. Whisk until just mixed. Add the melted butter and lemon zest and stir until thoroughly combined. Cover with plastic wrap and let sit for 30 minutes.

2. Position a rack in the middle of the oven. Preheat the oven to 350°F (180°F). Butter a 6-cup (1.5 L) shallow baking dish or eight ½-cup (125 mL) ramekins.

3. Pour the batter into the baking dish (or fill each ramekin about three-quarters of the way). Spread a layer of cherries on top of the batter. Bake for 30 to 35 minutes (20 to 22 minutes if you are using ramekins), until golden brown and just set in the middle. Let sit for 10 minutes before serving.

4. To serve, dust with icing sugar and sprinkle with almonds, if using.

Spanish Custard

The ultimate dessert to have in Barcelona is definitely crema catalana, or Spanish custard. This silky smooth classic is similar to crème brûlée but creamier in texture and with subtle hints of cinnamon and orange. A crackly burnt-sugar layer lies on top of the creamy and gooey custard. It simply doesn't get any better than that. This recipe doesn't take long to make, and it's such an impressive dessert to bring to the table. It's the perfect ending to dinner with friends, especially after enjoying Barcelona's Paella (page 184).

2½ cups (625 mL) 2% milk

1 strip orange peel (about 2 inches/5 cm)

1 strip lemon peel (about 2 inches/5 cm)

2 cinnamon sticks

5 egg yolks

⅓ cup (75 mL) + 2 tablespoons (30 mL) superfine sugar, divided

2 tablespoons (30 mL) cornstarch

1. Have ready four 6-ounce (175 mL) ramekins or oven-safe cups.

2. In a medium saucepan, combine the milk, orange peel, lemon peel, and cinnamon. Slowly bring to a boil over medium-high heat. Remove from the heat, cover with a lid, and let steep for 10 minutes.

3. In a medium bowl, whisk together the egg yolks, ⅓ cup (75 mL) of the sugar, and the cornstarch until the mixture is pale yellow, about 2 minutes. Slowly pour the milk through a strainer over the egg mixture and whisk until smooth.

4. Pour the custard mixture back into the pot and simmer over low heat, stirring constantly, until the custard has thickened and coats the back of the spoon. Do not let it boil.

5. Pour the custard into the ramekins. Cover the ramekins, placing plastic wrap directly on the surface of the custard. This will prevent a skin from forming. Let sit in the fridge overnight.

6. Before serving, remove the plastic wrap. Evenly sprinkle 1½ teaspoons (7 mL) of the sugar on top of each custard. (Tilting the ramekins in all directions helps distribute the sugar evenly.)

7. Using a small kitchen torch, caramelize the sugar, about 30 seconds. Or position a rack in the highest position and preheat the broiler to 500°F (260°C). Place the ramekins on a baking sheet and broil for 1½ minutes, or until the sugar is melted, golden brown, and bubbling.

Coconut Flan

1 cup (250 mL) granulated
  sugar
5 eggs
1 can (14 ounces/400 mL)
  full-fat coconut milk
1 can (14 ounces/400 mL)
  sweetened condensed milk
1 can (12 ounces/354 mL)
  evaporated milk
1 tablespoon (15 mL) pure
  vanilla extract
1 teaspoon (5 mL) white rum
1 cup (250 mL) sliced fresh
  strawberries

If you visit any South American country, or any of the islands in the Caribbean that were colonized by Spain, you'll be able to enjoy the ultimate custardy dessert. Flan, a silky mixture of eggs, sugar, and milk, gets baked in a *bain-marie,* or water bath, until it sets and picks up the flavours from the caramel underneath it. When I was growing up in Santo Domingo, every celebration, birthday, and Sunday lunch would end with a delicious flan.

This flan is made with creamy coconut milk, which makes the custard velvety smooth while adding a rich tropical flavour. Having just a few ingredients, it's also incredibly easy to make. Serve this super-delicate dessert at your next weekend lunch and be transported straight to the Caribbean!

1. Position a rack in the middle of the oven. Preheat the oven to 325°F (160°C).

2. Pour the sugar into a large frying pan. With a rubber spatula, stir constantly over medium heat while the sugar melts and turns a golden-brown caramel. If the sugar is browning too fast, reduce the heat to medium-low.

3. Immediately pour the caramel into a 9-inch (23 cm) flan pan or round baking dish, tilting the dish as you pour so that the caramel coats the bottom and sides of the pan. Work quickly because the caramel will start to set. Set aside.

4. In a large bowl, whisk the eggs, then whisk in the coconut milk, condensed milk, evaporated milk, vanilla, and rum. (Or you can combine all the ingredients in a blender and whirl for 30 seconds, until combined.) Pour the custard mixture over the cooled caramel.

5. Prepare a water bath by placing the flan pan in a larger baking dish (or roasting pan). Slide the baking dish into the oven and then pour enough hot water into the dish to come about halfway up the side (about 2 inches/5 cm) of the flan pan. Bake for 1 hour or until a toothpick inserted in the centre of the flan comes out clean.

continued

6. Remove the water bath from the oven and transfer the flan to a rack to cool completely. Store the flan overnight in the fridge, loosely covered with plastic wrap.

7. When ready to serve, set the flan on a baking sheet filled with ½ inch (1 cm) of hot water for 5 minutes. This will make it easier to unmould the flan.

8. To serve, run a knife around the sides of the flan to loosen it. Place a large round platter with a rim over the flan and invert it, allowing the flan to drop onto the platter and the caramel sauce to flow over and around the custard. Scatter a few sliced strawberries on top. Store, covered, in the fridge for up to 4 days.

Salted Caramel and Vanilla Bean Pots de Crème

Serves 8

Pots de Crème

4 tablespoons (60 mL/55 g) unsalted butter (½ stick)

¾ cup (175 mL) firmly packed brown sugar

½ teaspoon (2 mL) sea salt

½ vanilla bean, split lengthwise and seeds scraped (or 2 teaspoons/ 10 mL pure vanilla extract)

1¾ cups (425 mL) whipping (35%) cream

¾ cup (175 mL) 2% milk

6 egg yolks, at room temperature

1 tablespoon (15 mL) flaky sea salt (I use Maldon), for serving

Maple Whipped Cream

¼ cup (60 mL) whipping (35%) cream

1 tablespoon (15 mL) pure maple syrup

If you need a luscious and impressive dessert to serve for a dinner party, look no further than these salted caramel pots de crème. This classic dessert originated in France but can be easily baked in any kitchen. I started baking pots de crème after eating my first one at pastry school. I was instantly smitten with its silky texture and how versatile these creamy pots are. Chocolate is the most common flavour, but during a trip to Paris, I tried the most delicious salted caramel pots de crème, sprinkled with a pinch of sea salt flakes and a spoonful of freshly whipped cream. This recipe is proof that outstanding desserts can be made with just a handful of ingredients.

1. To make the pots de crème: Position a rack in the middle of the oven. Preheat the oven to 325°F (160°C). Have ready eight 6-ounce (175 mL) ramekins, oven-safe cups, or wide-mouth glass jars.

2. In a medium, heavy saucepan, melt the butter over medium heat. Add the brown sugar, salt, and vanilla seeds and whisk constantly for 5 minutes, or until the mixture is thick and a deep caramel colour.

3. Reduce the heat to medium-low. Whisking constantly, slowly add the cream (the mixture will bubble and the sugar will harden). Continue to whisk for 5 minutes, until the hardened sugar dissolves and the mixture starts to boil. Remove the pan from the heat and whisk in the milk.

4. In a large bowl, whisk the egg yolks. Gradually whisk in the caramel mixture. Strain the custard through a fine-mesh sieve into a 4-cup (1 L) liquid measuring cup or a medium bowl with a spout for easy pouring.

5. Pour the custard into the ramekins and transfer the ramekins to a shallow baking pan. Cover the baking pan with foil, leaving one corner uncovered. Slide the baking pan into the oven and carefully pour enough hot water into the pan to come halfway up the sides of the ramekins. Cover the open corner with the foil.

continued

6. Bake for 50 minutes, or until the custards are set around the edges and the centre jiggles slightly when the ramekins are gently shaken. Be very careful when lifting the foil; hot steam will escape out.

7. Using kitchen tongs, remove the ramekins from the hot water and transfer to a rack to cool for 1 hour. Cover with plastic wrap and refrigerate until chilled, at least 4 hours or ideally overnight.

8. When ready to serve, make the maple whipped cream: Beat the cream with the maple syrup until soft peaks form.

9. Sprinkle each pot de crème with a pinch of salt flakes and spoon about 1 tablespoon (15 mL) of whipped cream on top. Alternatively, you can use your favourite pastry tip and pipe the whipped cream on top.

Birthday Cheesecake

Makes 1 cheesecake,
Serves 8 to 10

Graham Crust

1½ cups (375 mL) graham
    cracker crumbs

3 tablespoons (45 mL)
    granulated sugar

1 tablespoon (15 mL)
    cinnamon

½ cup (125 mL/110 g) unsalted
    butter (1 stick), melted

Cream Cheese Filling

4 packages (8 ounces/250 g
    each) cream cheese, at room
    temperature

3 tablespoons (45 mL)
    all-purpose flour

¼ teaspoon (1 mL) sea salt

1¼ cups (300 mL) granulated
    sugar

½ cup (125 mL) full-fat sour
    cream

1 vanilla bean, split lengthwise
    and seeds scraped
    (or 1 tablespoon/15 mL pure
    vanilla extract)

3 eggs

During my countless trips to New York City, strolls in Central Park for some reason always leave me hungry, so I tend to go looking for cheesecake—one of the desserts I love most. In New York they are usually baked in a water bath and left plain (or topped minimally with strawberries), and rightfully so, as New York–style cheesecakes are famous for a reason. They are deliciously creamy, with speckles of vanilla throughout, and once you have a slice, it's impossible to visit New York and not have a piece.

At home, this cheesecake is how we celebrate birthdays. Isabella, my eldest daughter, likes hers topped with berries and raspberry coulis; when Gaby feels like switching from her usual chocolate cake with raspberries, she prefers her cheesecake topped with dulce de leche. Warren likes his cheesecake with Nutella and strawberries. This recipe is the one I've followed for years—a tradition as sweet as they come.

1. Position a rack in the middle of the oven. Preheat the oven to 300°F (150°F).

2. To make the graham crust: In a medium bowl, stir together the graham cracker crumbs, sugar, and cinnamon. Add the butter and stir with a fork until the mixture has absorbed the butter.

3. Scrape the crumb mixture into a 9-inch (23 cm) springform pan. With the bottom of a glass, press the crumbs evenly over the bottom and 2 inches (5 cm) up the sides of the pan. Press firmly to make a solid, even layer. Bake the crust for 8 minutes, or until fragrant and lightly brown. Set on a rack to cool.

4. Reduce the oven temperature to 250°F (120°C). Line a baking sheet with foil and place it on the lowest rack in the oven. The tray will catch any oils that drip from the cheesecake pan while baking.

5. To make the cream cheese filling: In a large bowl, using an electric mixer, beat the cream cheese, flour, and salt on medium speed until fluffy and smooth, about 3 minutes.

continued

Raspberry Sauce

1½ cups (375 mL) fresh
  raspberries
⅓ cup (75 mL) water
3 tablespoons (45 mL) pure
  maple syrup
Juice of ½ lemon
1 tablespoon + 1½ teaspoons
  (22 mL) cornstarch

Topping

2½ cups (625 mL) mixed fresh
  berries (such as strawberries,
  blackberries, blueberries,
  raspberries)

Turn off the mixer and scrape down the sides and bottom of the bowl with a rubber spatula.

6. Add the sugar, sour cream, and vanilla seeds and beat on medium speed until combined. Scrape down the sides of the bowl. Add the eggs, one at a time, beating well on medium-high speed after each egg is added.

7. Pour the filling into the crust. Bake until the centre of the cheesecake jiggles slightly when the pan is nudged, 65 to 70 minutes.

8. Carefully transfer the cheesecake to a rack and let cool completely. Cover with plastic wrap and refrigerate overnight.

9. To make the raspberry sauce: In a medium bowl, combine the raspberries, water, maple syrup, and lemon juice. Using an immersion blender, blend until smooth. Pour the mixture into a small saucepan. Add the cornstarch and stir with a whisk until dissolved. Cook over medium heat, stirring with a wooden spoon, until the sauce is thick enough to coat the back of the spoon. Remove from the heat and pour into a glass jar. Let cool to room temperature. Refrigerate until ready to serve the cheesecake.

10. To serve, remove the sides of the springform pan and place the cheesecake on a large plate or cake stand. Pour the raspberry sauce on top and decorate with berries. Store, covered, in the fridge for up to 4 days.

Citrus Bundt Cake

Makes 1 bundt cake, Serves 12

The Gràcia neighbourhood of Barcelona is where you can find some of the city's best bakeries. Some of them have been owned and operated by the same family for years. The breads and pastries have a homemade quality to them, which makes the whole experience of walking into one of these bakeries such a joy. It was at a bakery in Gràcia where I tried a delicious cake made with Valencia oranges. The cake, the owner told me, had been soaking in a citrus syrup overnight, infusing it with a wonderfully intoxicating fragrance that was in every tender crumb.

Back home, I made my version with navel oranges and lemons that my daughters love, and it won their seal of approval. Both the zest and the juice are used in this cake, which makes it burst with bright citrus flavours, while the buttermilk keeps it perfectly moist. I suggest you have a slice as soon as the cake has cooled for a bit.

Citrus Bundt Cake

3 cups (750 mL) cake flour, sifted

1 teaspoon (5 mL) salt

½ teaspoon (2 mL) baking powder

½ teaspoon (2 mL) baking soda

1 cup (250 mL/220 g) unsalted butter (2 sticks), at room temperature

1⅔ cups (400 mL) granulated sugar

4 eggs, at room temperature

2 teaspoons (10 mL) pure vanilla extract

¼ cup (60 mL) orange zest (about 3 oranges)

2 tablespoons (30 mL) lemon zest (about 2 lemons)

½ cup (125 mL) fresh orange juice (about 2 oranges)

¾ cup (175 mL) buttermilk, at room temperature, well shaken

1. Position a rack in the middle of the oven. Preheat the oven to 350°F (180°C). Generously spray a 10-inch (3 L) bundt pan with nonstick baking spray or grease with butter.

2. To make the citrus bundt cake: In a large bowl, whisk together the flour, salt, baking powder, and baking soda. Set aside.

3. In a large bowl using an electric mixer, or in a stand mixer fitted with the paddle attachment, beat the butter on high speed for about 2 minutes, until smooth and creamy. Add the sugar and beat on high speed until light and fluffy, about 2 minutes. Scrape down the sides and bottom of the bowl with a rubber spatula as needed.

4. Add the eggs and vanilla. Beat on medium-high speed until combined and the mixture looks glossy.

5. Add the orange and lemon zest and beat on medium speed until combined, about 1 minute. Pour in the orange juice and beat for 30 seconds. The mixture will look curdled, but it will come together once the dry ingredients are mixed in.

continued

Citrus Glaze

1¼ cups (300 mL) icing sugar, sifted

3 tablespoons (45 mL) fresh orange juice, more for a thinner consistency

½ teaspoon (2 mL) pure vanilla extract

Zest of 1 navel orange

Zest of 1 lemon

6. With the mixer on low speed, tip in the flour mixture in 3 additions, alternating with the buttermilk in 2 additions, and mixing after each addition just until combined. Do not overmix. The batter will be slightly thick.

7. Scrape the batter into the prepared pan. Bake for 45 to 50 minutes, or until a toothpick inserted into the centre of the cake comes out clean. If the top of the cake is browning too quickly, cover loosely with foil. Let cool in the pan on a rack for 10 minutes.

8. Invert the slightly cooled cake onto a rack set over a baking sheet. Let the cake cool for 30 minutes.

9. To make the citrus glaze: In a medium bowl, whisk together the icing sugar, orange juice, vanilla, orange zest, and lemon zest. Add 1 tablespoon (15 mL) of orange juice for a thinner consistency, if desired.

10. Drizzle the citrus glaze over the cake. Store, covered, at room temperature for up to 3 days or in the freezer (without the glaze) for up to 1 month.

Coconut Tres Leches Cake

Cake

1½ cups (375 mL) cake flour

1 teaspoon (5 mL) baking
  powder

½ teaspoon (2 mL) sea salt

½ cup (125 mL/110 g) unsalted
  butter (1 stick), at room
  temperature

1 cup + 2 tablespoons
  (280 mL) granulated sugar

5 eggs, at room temperature

1½ teaspoons (7 mL) pure
  vanilla extract

If you stop by a bakery in Mexico or Dominican Republic, you will very likely find a cake that's a bit unusual, but is it ever delicious! A vanilla sponge cake gets soaked in a creamy mixture of three milks—*tres leches*—and refrigerated overnight to let all that goodness soak in, then it is topped with glossy meringue or whipped cream. It's a celebration cake often served at birthday parties and Sunday family lunches.

The three milks are usually whole milk, evaporated milk, and condensed milk, which infuse the cake with moisture and flavour. Honouring my Dominican roots, I swapped the whole milk for coconut milk, which gives the *tres leches* mixture a more tropical flavour. The whipped cream on top is flavoured with vanilla, but I've sweetened it with maple syrup instead of sugar for a touch of Canadian flair. This cake gets better as it sits in the fridge, so it can be made a few days ahead. It makes for a sweet ending to a summer barbecue. I've topped the cake with strawberries, but it is equally delicious with fresh mixed berries or sliced fresh peaches.

1. Position a rack in the middle of the oven. Preheat the oven to 350°F (180°C). Butter a 13- × 9-inch (3 L) baking pan.

2. To make the cake: In a medium bowl, whisk together the flour, baking powder, and salt.

3. Using an electric mixer, beat the butter in a large bowl on medium speed until smooth and creamy, about 1 minute. Turn the mixer down to low speed and gradually add the sugar, then mix for 1 minute. Stop to scrape down the sides of the bowl if needed.

4. Add the eggs one at a time, mixing until well blended after each addition. Mix in the vanilla. Add the flour mixture in 3 additions, mixing after each addition just until combined.

5. Scrape the batter into the prepared pan and spread it evenly. It will appear to be a very small amount of batter, but it rises while baking. Bake until the cake is light golden and a toothpick inserted in the centre comes out clean, 22 to 24 minutes.

continued

Tres Leches Sauce

1 can (14 ounces/400 mL)
coconut milk

1 can (14 ounces/400 mL)
sweetened condensed milk

1 can (12 ounces/354 mL)
evaporated milk

½ teaspoon (2 mL) pure
vanilla extract

Maple Whipped Cream

2 cups (500 mL) whipping
(35%) cream

¼ cup (60 mL) pure maple
syrup

1 teaspoon (5 mL) pure vanilla
extract

2 cups (500 mL) sliced fresh
strawberries, for serving

6. Transfer the pan to a rack and let cool for 30 minutes. Using a fork, poke holes all over the top of the cake, then cool completely.

7. To make the tres leches sauce: In a 4-cup (1 L) measuring cup or a medium bowl with a spout, whisk together the coconut milk, condensed milk, evaporated milk, and vanilla. Slowly pour the sauce over the cake. Cover the pan with plastic wrap and refrigerate the cake for at least 6 hours or overnight. The sauce absorbs better if the cake soaks overnight.

8. Just before serving, make the maple whipped cream: Using an electric mixer, beat the cream, maple syrup, and vanilla in a large bowl on high speed until stiff peaks form. Spread the whipped cream over the cake. Top the cake with sliced strawberries and serve. Store the cake, covered with plastic wrap, in the fridge for up to 4 days.

Chocolate and Raspberry Cake

My daughters and I have lived in three different countries. Birthdays have been celebrated in each, but the one thing that never changes is this delicious chocolate and raspberry cake. Like mother, like daughter, chocolate is Gaby's flavour of choice when it comes to cakes, and nothing makes me happier than to celebrate my youngest with her favourite birthday treat. The raspberry filling and fresh berries on top of the cake balance the richness of the chocolate, the crumb is soft, and the icing is smooth and velvety, making this a cake to be baked not only for a birthday but to take to a friend's house for dinner. Made to put a smile on your face.

Chocolate Cake

2 cups (500 mL) granulated sugar

1¾ cups (425 mL) all-purpose flour

¾ cup (175 mL) cocoa powder

2 teaspoons (10 mL) baking soda

1 teaspoon (5 mL) baking powder

1 teaspoon (5 mL) sea salt

½ teaspoon (2 mL) cinnamon

2 eggs, at room temperature

1 cup (250 mL) buttermilk, at room temperature, well shaken

½ cup (125 mL) canola oil

1½ teaspoons (7 mL) pure vanilla extract

½ cup (125 mL) hot water

½ cup (125 mL) hot coffee

Raspberry Filling

2 cups (500 mL) fresh or thawed frozen raspberries, divided

½ cup + 1 tablespoon (140 mL) water

2 tablespoons (30 mL) pure maple syrup

1. Position a rack in the middle of the oven. Preheat the oven to 350°F (180°C). Butter two 8-inch (20 cm) round cake pans, line the bottoms with parchment paper, and butter and flour the parchment paper.

2. To make the chocolate cake: In the bowl of a stand mixer, sift together the sugar, flour, cocoa, baking soda, baking powder, salt, and cinnamon. Attach the paddle attachment and mix on low speed until combined.

3. Add the eggs, buttermilk, canola oil, and vanilla. Mix on low speed for 1 minute. Pour in the hot water and coffee and mix on low speed for 1 minute, scraping the sides and bottom of the bowl with a rubber spatula as necessary. The batter will look glossy and quite thin.

4. Divide the batter evenly between the prepared pans. Bake for 35 minutes, or until a toothpick inserted in the centre of the cake comes out clean and the cake has pulled away from the sides slightly.

5. Cool in the pan on a rack for 20 minutes. Turn out the cakes onto a rack, remove the parchment paper, and let cool completely.

6. To make the raspberry filling: In a small bowl, combine 1½ cups (375 mL) of the raspberries, the water, and maple syrup. Using an immersion blender, blend until smooth.

continued

Chocolate Icing

6 ounces (170 g) semisweet
  chocolate, chopped (I use
  Valrhona)

1 cup (250 mL/220 g) unsalted
  butter (2 sticks), at room
  temperature

1 egg yolk, at room
  temperature

1½ teaspoons (7 mL) pure
  vanilla extract

1¼ cups (300 mL) icing sugar,
  sifted

Topping

2 cups (500 mL) mixed fresh
  berries (such as strawberries,
  blueberries, raspberries)

Cut the remaining ½ cup (125 mL) raspberries in half and set aside in a separate small bowl.

7. To make the chocolate icing: Place the chocolate in a heatproof bowl set over a pot filled with an inch or so of simmering water. Stir until the chocolate is melted. Remove from the heat and cool to room temperature.

8. In the cleaned bowl of the stand mixer fitted with the paddle attachment, beat the butter on medium-high speed until fluffy, about 4 minutes. Add the egg yolk and vanilla and continue beating for 3 minutes. Turn the mixer to low speed and slowly add the icing sugar. Then beat the mixture on medium speed until smooth and creamy, about 3 minutes, scraping down the sides of the bowl as needed.

9. Pour in the melted chocolate. Beat on medium-high speed for 2 minutes, until combined and creamy.

10. To assemble the cake: Place 1 cake layer flat side down on a plate or cake stand. With a fork, poke holes in the top of the cake, then spread the raspberry filling evenly over the cake. Scatter the reserved cut raspberries over the filling. Place the second cake layer on top, flat side down. With an offset spatula, spread the icing evenly over the top and sides of the cake.

11. Scatter the mixed berries over the top of the cake. (If using strawberries, cut a few in half before decorating the cake.) Enjoy immediately. This cake is best the day it is made but can be kept in a covered container at room temperature for up to 2 days.

French Yogurt Cake with Cherries

Makes 1 cake, Serves 8

1½ cups (375 mL) all-purpose
 flour
2 teaspoons (10 mL) baking
 powder
¾ teaspoon (4 mL) sea salt
1⅓ cups (325 mL) frozen pitted
 sweet cherries
1 cup (250 mL) granulated
 sugar
1 tablespoon (15 mL) finely
 grated lemon zest
¾ cup (175 mL) whole milk or
 plain full-fat Greek yogurt
½ cup (125 mL) canola oil
2 eggs, at room temperature
1 teaspoon (5 mL) pure
 almond extract

For serving

3 tablespoons (45 mL) icing
 sugar
Maple Vanilla Whipped Cream
 (page 47)

I first tried yogurt cake while attending Le Cordon Bleu in Mexico City. Cedric, our teacher and *pâtissier*, would often bake a few yogurt cakes while students worked on opera cakes, bûches de Noël, mille-feuille, and macarons. He wanted us to try a simpler way of baking, not one of the French classics but the kind of baking that brings back memories of cakes made at home, on a rainy day, on a weekend.

The French yogurt cake, as we named it in class, soon became a ritual. Cedric would present one at the end of the day when our aprons told the story of seven hours of baking those iconic classic desserts. Warm out of the oven and with the occasional teaspoon of preserves spread on top, it was the sweetest way to end our day. I've always treasured those memories, and I still bake my own version of yogurt cake at home. In the summer, I love adding cherries and a dash of almond extract to the batter.

1. Position a rack in the middle of the oven. Preheat the oven to 350°F (180°C). Generously spray an 8-inch (20 cm) round cake pan with nonstick baking spray.

2. In a medium bowl, whisk together the flour, baking powder, and salt. Stir in the frozen cherries.

3. In another medium bowl, whisk together the granulated sugar, lemon zest, yogurt, canola oil, eggs, and almond extract. Fold in the flour mixture until just blended.

4. Pour the batter into the prepared pan, spreading it evenly. Bake for 50 to 55 minutes, until the top is golden brown and a toothpick inserted in the centre of the cake comes out clean.

5. Let the cake cool in the pan on a rack for 15 minutes. Invert the cake onto a rack and let cool completely. Once cooled, turn the cake right way up. Carefully sift the icing sugar over the cake.

6. Slice the cake and serve with a generous dollop of maple whipped cream. The cake is best the day it is made but can be stored, covered at room temperature, for up to 3 days or in the freezer for up to 1 month.

Chocolate Truffles with Cocoa and Pistachios

Makes 20 truffles

1¼ cups (300 mL) whipping (35%) cream
⅛ teaspoon (0.5 mL) sea salt
12 ounces (340 g) bittersweet or semisweet chocolate, finely chopped
1 cup (250 mL) raw pistachios, toasted and finely chopped
¼ cup (60 mL) cocoa powder

My first trip to Paris was majorly planned around food. I also wanted to explore Le Marais and St. Germain and get lost in the winding and hilly streets of Montmartre. Armed with a page-long list of bakeries, cafés, and restaurants, Warren and I started eating our way through Paris. One of the best memories from that trip was walking into the beautifully designed L'Atelier de l'Éclair (now closed) and finding chocolates filled with smooth ganache and melt-in-your-mouth truffles delicately rolled in cocoa powder and crushed nuts. I came back to Toronto in love with the City of Lights and its stunning architecture, café culture, and memorable pastries.

The quality of the chocolate you use in these truffles is extremely important. I suggest either Valrhona or Callebaut. This recipe is very flexible; you can switch pistachios for hazelnuts, pecans, or any nut you like as long as the pieces are small. You can also add a tablespoon of your favourite liqueur to the chocolate ganache, or a pinch of ground cinnamon, or you could steep Earl Grey tea in the cream to flavour it.

1. In a medium saucepan, bring the cream and salt to a boil over medium heat. Remove from the heat, add the chocolate, and whisk until smooth and glossy.

2. Pour the mixture into a medium bowl and let cool to room temperature. Cover with plastic wrap and refrigerate until firm, 2 to 3 hours.

3. Place the pistachios in a shallow bowl. Place the cocoa in another shallow bowl.

4. Working quickly, roll a rounded 1 teaspoon (6 mL) of the chocolate mixture into a 1-inch (2.5 cm) ball using your hands. Roll the truffle in the pistachios to coat, then roll in the cocoa to coat. Repeat to coat the remaining truffles.

5. Store the truffles between layers of wax paper in a covered container in the fridge for up to 1 week. Let the truffles stand at room temperature for about 5 minutes before serving.

Lemon and Coconut Tart

Makes 1 tart, Serves 8

Pastry

2 cups (500 mL) all-purpose
    flour

3 tablespoons (45 mL)
    granulated sugar

½ cup (125 mL/110 g) very cold
    butter (1 stick), cubed

2 to 3 tablespoons (30 to 45 mL)
    ice water

Lemon and Coconut Filling

¾ cup (175 mL) fresh lemon
    juice

¾ cup (175 mL) granulated
    sugar

¾ cup (175 mL) whipping (35%)
    cream

1 tablespoon (15 mL) pure
    coconut extract

3 eggs, lightly beaten

Lemon desserts have always reminded me of summer and the beauty of the Amalfi Coast, from *dolce di Amalfi*, a fragrant almond and lemon cake, to *delizie al limone*, a light sponge cake filled with lemon cream, brushed with limoncello syrup, and covered in a lemon whipped cream.

I live close to Toronto, a city full of great bakeries where odds are you will find a classic lemon blueberry tart. But if you want to try something different, then this lemon and coconut tart is for you. The coconut flavour adds delightful sweetness to balance the tanginess of the lemons and gives the tart a tropical flair. Top it with freshly whipped cream, berries, and toasted coconut chips for a true taste of summer on a plate.

1. To make the pastry: In a food processor, combine the flour, sugar, and butter. Pulse until the mixture resembles fine breadcrumbs. With the motor running, add just enough ice water to form a smooth dough.

2. Transfer the dough to a lightly floured work surface and shape into a circle. It's okay to knead it lightly to make the shape even. Wrap in plastic wrap and refrigerate for 30 minutes.

3. On a lightly floured surface and using a lightly floured rolling pin, roll the dough into a 13-inch (33 cm) circle, about ⅛ inch (3 mm) thick. Carefully lift one edge of the dough and roll the dough loosely around the rolling pin. Unroll the dough over a 9-inch (23 cm) fluted tart tin with removable bottom and carefully press it with your fingers around the bottom and into the sides of the pan. Using a sharp paring knife, trim any overhanging dough and discard. Prick the bottom of the pastry all over with a fork. Cover with plastic wrap and freeze for 30 minutes.

4. Position a rack in the middle of the oven. Preheat the oven to 350°F (180°C).

continued

Maple Whipped Cream

1 cup (250 mL) whipping (35%) cream

2 teaspoons (10 mL) pure maple syrup

1 teaspoon (5 mL) pure coconut extract

Toppings

1 cup (250 mL) mixed fresh berries (such as strawberries, raspberries, blueberries, red currants)

1 cup (250 mL) natural coconut chips

Icing sugar, for dusting (optional)

5. Press a piece of parchment paper into the tart shell. Fill it with baking weights or large uncooked beans or rice. Place the tart tin on a baking sheet. Bake for 10 minutes. Remove the weights or beans and bake for an additional 10 minutes, or until the pastry is light golden. Remove the tart shell from the oven, set aside, and reduce the oven temperature to 300°F (150°C).

6. To make the lemon and coconut filling: Combine the lemon juice and sugar in a heatproof bowl. Set the bowl over a pot filled with an inch or so of simmering water and stir until the sugar is dissolved and the mixture is warm. Add the cream, coconut extract, and eggs and stir constantly with a rubber spatula for 5 minutes, or until the mixture is thick enough that it sticks to the back of a spoon.

7. Using a fine-mesh sieve, strain the lemon and coconut mixture into the tart shell. Bake for 22 to 24 minutes, until the filling is just set. It should jiggle a bit in the centre. Let cool on a rack for 30 minutes.

8. To make the maple whipped cream and assemble: Beat the cream with the maple syrup and coconut extract until soft peaks form. Using a piping bag fitted with a decorative tip (I use a Wilton 1B drop flower tip), pipe the whipped cream onto one side of the tart. Scatter the berries and coconut flakes along the same side of the tart. Dust with icing sugar, if using. The tart can be stored (without the toppings), covered, in the fridge for up to 2 days.

Chocolate Tart with Strawberries and Cream

Makes 1 tart, Serves 6

Pastry

½ cup (125 mL) icing sugar

¼ cup (60 mL) raw pecans, toasted

¾ cup (175 mL) all-purpose flour

¼ cup (60 mL) cocoa powder

¼ teaspoon (1 mL) sea salt

½ cup (125 mL/110 g) cold unsalted butter (1 stick), cut into small pieces

Filling

14 ounces (400 g) bittersweet or semisweet chocolate, chopped

6 tablespoons (90 mL) unsalted butter

2 eggs, lightly beaten

¼ cup (60 mL) granulated sugar

1 teaspoon (5 mL) pure vanilla extract

I've always been a chocolate lover. One of my fondest memories growing up was going with my mom for a slice of chocolate cake after piano lessons. The bakery was in the historic old part of Santo Domingo, where cobblestone streets lined with lush trees cascading onto each other made for such a perfect view. Sharing a slice of that fudgy chocolate cake layered with vanilla buttercream was how my love for chocolate started. Years later, while attending pastry school and having fallen for the art of tart making, I experimented, using different spices to enhance the flavour of the chocolate, be it chili powder, cinnamon, or cardamom. I tested countless recipes, but it is now this chocolate tart, served with strawberries and cream, that I go back to over and over for its creamy filling and crumbly crust.

Good-quality chocolate is a must in this recipe, and if you fear rolling out tart dough into a tin, then this recipe is for you, as the crust instead gets pressed into the tin, making it the easiest tart you'll ever make.

1. Position a rack in the middle of the oven. Preheat the oven to 350°F (180°C). Lightly butter an 11-inch (28 cm) fluted tart tin with removable bottom.

2. To make the pastry: In a food processor, combine the icing sugar and pecans and process until the pecans are finely ground. Add the flour, cocoa, and salt. Pulse just until blended. Drop in the butter. Pulse just until the mixture begins to come together when a small amount of the dough is pressed between your fingers. Do not overprocess: the mixture should not become a ball.

3. Press the dough evenly into the bottom and up the sides of the tart pan. Trim any overhang and prick the dough all over with a fork. Cover in plastic wrap and freeze for 30 minutes.

4. Place the tart pan on a baking sheet. Bake until the pastry is fragrant, starts to pull away from the sides of the pan, and

continued

Toppings

¼ cup (60 mL) cocoa powder, for dusting

¾ cup (175 mL) whipping (35%) cream

1 tablespoon (15 mL) granulated sugar

1½ cups (375 mL) sliced fresh strawberries

is a deep chocolate-brown colour, 15 to 18 minutes. Let cool on a rack while you make the filling.

5. To make the filling: In a heatproof bowl set over a pot filled with an inch or so of simmering water, melt the chocolate with the butter, whisking until smooth. Remove the bowl from the heat and let cool for 5 minutes. Whisk in the eggs and granulated sugar until blended. Whisk in the vanilla. Pour the filling into the warm crust.

6. Bake for about 12 minutes, until the filling is set around the edges but slightly jiggly in the centre; the top of the tart will look a bit blistered, and that's okay. Transfer to a rack to cool completely, at least 1½ hours.

7. To make the topping and assemble: Dust the top the tart with cocoa powder. Beat together the cream and granulated sugar until soft peaks form. Spoon about ½ cup (125 mL) of the whipped cream onto the middle of the tart. Cover the cream with a few sliced strawberries. Serve each slice with additional cream and sliced strawberries. Store the tart (without the whipped cream), covered, in the fridge for up to 2 days.

Fudgiest Chocolate Brownies with Salted Caramel Sauce

Makes 16 brownies

Fudgiest Chocolate Brownies

1½ cups (375 mL/330 g)
  unsalted butter (3 sticks)

3 ounces (85 g) unsweetened
  chocolate, coarsely chopped

3 eggs, at room temperature

1½ cups (375 mL) granulated
  sugar

1 teaspoon (5 mL) pure vanilla
  extract

1 cup (250 mL) all-purpose
  flour

¾ teaspoon (4 mL) sea salt

1 cup (250 mL) semisweet
  chocolate chips or chopped
  semisweet chocolate

Salted Caramel Sauce

1 cup (250 mL) granulated
  sugar

6 tablespoons (90 mL)
  unsalted butter, cut into
  pieces

½ cup (125 mL) whipping (35%)
  cream

1 teaspoon (5 mL) sea salt

Vanilla ice cream, for serving

On a trip to San Francisco with my friend Amy and our daughters, the girls wanted to stop at the Ghirardelli chocolate store, and who could blame them? For kids and grown-ups alike, it's a chocolate lover's paradise. That day we picked a few of our favourites, including their salted caramel chocolates. We had a few on the spot because quite honestly it was pretty hard to resist. Those little squares were the perfect combination of salty and sweet and brought memories of ice cream sundaes on a hot summer's day and of fudgy brownies. I came home from that trip inspired to bake a few desserts with chocolate, and that's how this recipe was born. If you like moist, chewy brownies, this recipe is for you. Top a warm square with your favourite vanilla ice cream and drizzle with a spoonful of salted caramel sauce for a luscious dessert.

1. Position a rack in the middle of the oven. Preheat the oven to 375°F (190°C). Lightly butter an 8-inch (2 L) square baking pan and line the bottom and sides with parchment paper, leaving an overhang to use as handles to remove the brownies from the pan.

2. To make the fudgiest chocolate brownies: In a heatproof bowl set over a medium pot filled with an inch or so of simmering water, stir the butter and chocolate with a rubber spatula until the mixture is completely melted and combined. Remove the pan from the heat but keep the bowl over the water to keep the mixture warm. This will also give the brownies a shiny, crackly top.

3. In a large bowl, whisk together the eggs, sugar, and vanilla.

4. In a medium bowl, sift together the flour and salt.

5. Pour the warm chocolate mixture slowly over the egg mixture, whisking until incorporated. With a rubber spatula, quickly fold in the flour mixture. Fold in the chocolate chips.

6. Immediately pour the mixture into the prepared baking pan, spreading it evenly. Bake for 10 minutes. Rotate the

continued

pan and bake for another 10 minutes, or until the brownies are shiny and crackly on top.

7. Transfer the pan to a rack and let cool completely. Using the parchment paper overhang, lift the brownies from the pan and place on a cutting board. Cut into 2-inch (5 cm) squares.

8. To make the salted caramel sauce: In a medium saucepan, heat the sugar over medium heat, stirring constantly with a heatproof rubber spatula. The sugar will form clumps but will eventually melt into a thick caramel as you continue to stir. Be careful that it doesn't burn.

9. Once the sugar is completely melted and the caramel is thick and amber coloured, carefully add the butter. The caramel will bubble rapidly when the butter is added. Using a whisk, stir in the butter until it is completely melted, about 2 minutes.

10. While stirring, very slowly drizzle in the cream. Since the cream is cold, the mixture will bubble and splatter. Boil for 1 minute. Remove from the heat and stir in the salt. Transfer to a glass jar and set on a rack to cool.

11. To serve the brownies, top each square with a scoop of vanilla ice cream and drizzle 2 tablespoons (30 mL) of the salted caramel sauce on top.

12. Store the brownies in an airtight container at room temperature for up to 2 days or in the freezer, individually wrapped in plastic, for up to 1 month. When ready to serve, unwrap and heat in the oven at 300°F (150°C) for about 5 minutes. Store the salted caramel sauce, covered tightly, in the fridge for up to 2 weeks. Reheat in the microwave on High for 20 seconds before using.

Churros with Chocolate Cinnamon Sauce

Chocolate Cinnamon Sauce

1 cup (250 mL) whipping (35%) cream

½ vanilla bean, split lengthwise and seeds scraped (or 1 teaspoon/5 mL pure vanilla extract)

⅓ cup (75 mL) firmly packed dark brown sugar

1 tablespoon (15 mL) cocoa powder

½ teaspoon (2 mL) cinnamon

⅛ teaspoon (0.5 mL) sea salt

3 ounces (85 g) unsweetened chocolate, chopped

Churros

1 cup (250 mL) + 1 tablespoon (15 mL) granulated sugar, divided

1 tablespoon + 1½ teaspoons (22 mL) cinnamon

½ cup (125 mL) 2% milk

½ cup (125 mL) water

6 tablespoons (90 mL) unsalted butter

1 teaspoon (5 mL) sea salt

1 cup (250 mL) all-purpose flour

3 eggs, at room temperature

10 cups (2.5 L) vegetable oil (approx.), for frying

When I was a child, a dear friend of the family would visit and bring us a bag filled with hot churros. Dusted in cinnamon sugar, these were the ultimate treat and the beginning of my love for this crispy pastry. This dessert gets made all over Latin America and Spain. I've had churros with cinnamon-scented hot chocolate sauce in Buenos Aires and Madrid, dusted with icing sugar in Mexico City, and with a thick caramel sauce in Barcelona.

These churros with chocolate sauce are very easy to make, but make sure to use a star-shaped (not round) pastry tip to pipe them. The outside is deliciously crispy, but the churros remain soft inside. Dipped in the rich chocolate cinnamon sauce, these will find the way to your heart in no time.

1. To make the chocolate cinnamon sauce: In a small saucepan, combine the cream and vanilla seeds over medium heat for 1 minute. Stir in the brown sugar, cocoa, cinnamon, and salt. Bring to a simmer over medium-high heat, whisking occasionally, until the sugar is dissolved, no lumps of cocoa remain, and the mixture is simmering, about 4 minutes. Remove from the heat. Add the chocolate and stir until melted. Keep the sauce warm over very low heat until ready to serve.

2. To make the churros: Fit a pastry bag with a medium star tip (I use an Ateco 845 tip) and set aside. In a medium bowl, whisk together 1 cup (250 mL) of the granulated sugar and the cinnamon. Transfer the sugar mixture to a large plate.

3. In a medium saucepan, combine the milk, water, butter, salt, and the remaining 1 tablespoon (15 mL) granulated sugar. Bring to a simmer over medium-high heat.

4. Add the flour all at once and vigorously stir with a wooden spoon until the dough comes together, about 30 seconds. Transfer to the bowl of a stand mixer fitted with the paddle attachment (or a large bowl). Let cool slightly.

continued

5. With the mixer on medium-low speed, stir in the eggs, one at a time, making sure each egg is incorporated before adding the next (or beat in with a wooden spoon). The dough will look curdled at first, but continue to beat, scraping the sides of the bowl occasionally, until the dough comes together and is smooth and glossy. Spoon the dough into the prepared pastry bag.

6. Line a baking sheet with paper towel. Half fill a large, heavy pot with vegetable oil. Fit the pot with a deep-fry thermometer and heat the oil over medium-high heat to 350°F (180°C). Holding the pastry bag at an angle and with the tip a few inches above the oil, squeeze out dough, moving the bag as you squeeze so you pipe a 6-inch (15 cm) ribbon of dough. Using a paring knife, cut the dough at the piping tip. Repeat to make 4 more churros.

7. Fry the churros until golden brown, 2 to 3 minutes per side, turning once and adjusting the heat to maintain the oil temperature. Drain on the paper towels. Repeat with the remaining dough.

8. Roll the warm churros in the cinnamon sugar. Enjoy immediately, dipped in warm chocolate cinnamon sauce.

Poppy Seed and Vanilla Bean Madeleines

Makes 12 cookies

1 cup (250 mL) all-purpose
flour

1 teaspoon (5 mL) baking
powder

1 tablespoon (15 mL) poppy
seeds

⅔ cup (150 mL) butter, at room
temperature

5 eggs

1 cup (250 mL) granulated
sugar

½ vanilla bean, split lengthwise
and seeds scraped

Icing sugar, for dusting

Going into bakeries is one of the things I love to do the most while travelling. In Paris, you must stop at an Eric Kayser for their madeleines. Grab a few more than you intend to eat. Trust me when I say you'll be coming back for more—they are incredibly buttery, have that perfect golden crust, and melt in your mouth. But if you can't just zip off to Paris, these madeleines are just as delicious.

At home I make a few different types of madeleines, sometimes combining nuts and spices, or simply adding a bit of citrus zest, but it's the slight crunch of the poppy seeds and the fragrance of vanilla that make these madeleines the perfect little treat to have with tea or coffee after a leisurely brunch. Dust with icing sugar and enjoy them warm.

1. In a medium bowl, sift together the flour and baking powder. Add the poppy seeds and stir with a fork.

2. In a medium saucepan, melt the butter over medium-high heat and cook until slightly brown, about 5 minutes. Remove from the heat and let cool to room temperature.

3. In a medium bowl, whisk together the eggs and sugar until creamy and pale yellow, about 2 minutes. Whisk in the vanilla seeds until well incorporated.

4. Using a rubber spatula, fold the flour mixture into the egg mixture. Add the cooled melted butter through a fine-mesh sieve and fold it in.

5. You can bake the madeleines right away or cover with plastic wrap and let the batter rest in the fridge for a few hours or overnight. This will make the crust turn a slight caramel colour and allows the vanilla seeds to infuse the batter for longer, resulting in deliciously fragrant madeleines.

6. When ready to bake, position a rack in the middle of the oven. Preheat the oven to 350°F (180°C). Butter and flour a madeleine tin, then shake out any excess flour.

7. Fit a piping bag with a ½-inch (1 cm) plain tip. Place the bag tip down in a large glass and scrape the batter into the bag.

continued

(Alternatively, scrape the batter into a resealable plastic bag and snip off one corner.) Pipe the batter into each well in a straight motion, filling each well three-quarters full. Bake for 22 minutes, or until golden and a small dome has risen out of each madeleine.

8. Cool in the pan on a rack for 5 minutes. Tip out the madeleines and enjoy immediately, dusted with icing sugar. Store in a covered container at room temperature for up to 2 days or in the freezer for up to 1 month.

Tip Instead of poppy seed and vanilla, substitute any of these variations:

- ½ teaspoon (2 mL) ground cinnamon + 2 tablespoons (30 mL) finely chopped raw pecans

- 1 tablespoon (15 mL) lemon zest

- ½ teaspoon (2 mL) ground cardamom + 2 tablespoons (30 mL) finely chopped raw hazelnuts

Acknowledgments

This book is a dream come true. Little did I know when I started collecting cookbooks in Montreal that one day I would be given the chance to work on one of my own. It has truly been a labour of love, one that I've poured my soul into. And it wouldn't have been possible without the help and support of some of the kindest people I know.

To my parents, for your never-ending love, for teaching me the value of following my dreams, and for constantly being there for me even though we live miles apart. Thank you for always giving me the best advice. You have taught me so much about life, and I have no words to express how much I love you both.

To my daughters, Isabella and Gabriela, for always believing in me, giving me the sweetest hugs, and being so supportive during the making of this book. Thanks for being my inspiration and for keeping our Sunday waffles tradition strong. You mean everything to me and are my reason for being.

To my partner, Warren, for insisting I took breaks when he saw I needed them, for making sure I got in some workouts during this process, and for making me laugh on days I was a bit overwhelmed. The memories we create while sitting around the table with the girls are a treasure to me, and I am forever grateful for your presence in our lives. I love you.

To Isabella's dad, Todd, and his family, thank you for your unwavering support and kindness.

To my family in Dominican Republic, whose encouragement is so full of love. Thanks for always being present. Patricia, you are a sister to me.

To Monica Siccar, for being a second mom to me and driving all the way from Baltimore to Toronto to see us and support me with the book.

To Lauren McPhillips and Alexa Fernando, two of the most inspiring women I know and whom I'm honoured to call my friends. Your knowledge and support were instrumental while working on the book.

To my friends Pernille Petersen and Amy Beaulieu, for your generosity, words of support and kindness, and true friendship.

To Gloria Chick, for always hopping on the phone to make me laugh, and being willing to help.

To Sarah Miller and Rachelle Saevil, for helping bring my book proposal to life and spending time creating it with me.

To my amazing editor, Andrea Magyar, for giving me the opportunity to fulfill this dream and for believing in me. Your guidance, kindness, and support have helped make this book possible. Thank you from the bottom of my heart. I am forever grateful to the rest of the team at Penguin Random House Canada for this opportunity.

To Stacey Glick, my literary agent, for believing in this project and understanding my vision.

To my recipe testers, who had such an important part in creating this cookbook. Thank you for your generosity of time and feedback.

To my childhood friends Alina and Elizabeth, for being not only friends but true sisters to me.

Many thanks to the team at Shine PR, especially Jess Hunichen, Emily Ward, and Samantha Hicks, and everyone I've met during my travels.

To Geneva Moore, for the love and support you have given the girls and me since we met. We love being part of your family.

To Kam Siddiqui, Tara O'Brady, Laura Wright, and Jeanine Donofrio who, upon learning I was writing this cookbook, gave me priceless advice and encouragement.

Lastly, thank you to the readers of *Diala's Kitchen*, for making my recipes in your kitchens and creating your own food traditions. Your kindness has always meant so much to me.

Index